But She Looks Fine

From Illness to Activism

Olivia Goodreau

But She Looks Fine

From Illness to Activism

Foreword by
Colonel Nicole M.E. Malachowski, USAF, Retired

GAUDIUM

Gaudium Publishing

Las Vegas ♦ Chicago ♦ Palm Beach

Published in the United States of America by
Histria Books
7181 N. Hualapai Way, Ste. 130-86
Las Vegas, NV 89166 U.S.A.
HistriaBooks.com

Gaudium Publishing is an imprint of Histria Books. Titles published under the imprints of Histria Books are distributed worldwide.

Library of Congress Control Number: 2023932289

ISBN 978-1-59211-210-4 (hardcover)
ISBN 978-1-59211-419-1 (softbound)
ISBN 978-1-59211-356-9 (eBook)

Contents

Dedicated to
Kathy, Dr. Spector, and Jack and Will

Foreword

How can one teenage girl change the world?

I first met Olivia Goodreau when she was thirteen years old. She had just finished delivering a deeply moving and thoughtful speech to the inaugural working group at the headquarters of the Department of Health and Human Services in Washington, D.C. This working group included every high-level stakeholder in our community: academic researchers, medical providers, government policy-makers, patients and their caregivers. Her story had their rapt attention, as well as mine. I was so impressed and inspired, I had to meet her. At the time, I was a 43-year-old Air Force Colonel, a combat-proven fighter pilot, about to be unceremoniously medically retired from military service due to my own chronic illness. The truth is, in that moment, I was feeling angry, abandoned, betrayed, and hurt by the larger healthcare system. But thanks to Olivia, a true force of nature, I came away thinking, "We can change things for the better."

When I met Olivia that day, she approached me and got right to the point. I immediately admired her confidence and poise. She asked me if I would help her in the fight against the "invisible illness" we both were fighting. I couldn't say no. I answered, in my typical fighter-pilot language, "I would be happy to be your wingman. You're our flight lead." After 20+ years in the military, I'd learned how to recognize courage, skill, bravery, and leadership when I saw it. I wanted to be a part of whatever difficult mission she was on.

So, how does one teenage girl change the world? By being entrepreneurial, creative, and innovative. By being unafraid to go into the lion's den of bureaucracy, inertia, stigma, bias, and scarce resources. By taking situations that adults see as contentious and turning them into opportunities for collaboration. She's not distracted, despite the trauma she's endured; she's 100% secure in her truth and focused. She's a tireless and unstoppable voice for all the voiceless sufferers of invisible chronic illness. How can we not be moved that someone so young overcame so much, yet still made it through the worst and reclaimed her life? Despite all she still suffers, she is emotionally and mentally so strong. She shares her story with equal parts power and grace.

I know this book will leave every reader incredibly impressed and positively changed by Olivia Goodreau. More than that, however, Olivia's story has valuable lessons for all of us. It's a lesson in the power of self-advocacy to get access to the healthcare we deserve for ourselves, and then take that message forward to the collective. It's a lesson of how to be a trailblazer and move forward when momentum seems hopelessly stalled. It's a lesson in the power of family and friends to provide support and encouragement in the toughest of times. It's a lesson for policymakers and clinicians in understanding that each patient's experience is so much more than just part of a data set. By giving voice to the voiceless, Olivia reminds all of us that we have the power to live a life of significance and positive impact.

But She Looks Fine is a call to hope. In the long hard battle of any invisible chronic illness, it often seems that hope is all we have left. But we also have an entire army fighting with us and for us, and Olivia Goodreau is leading the charge.

Colonel Nicole M.E. Malachowski, USAF, Retired

1

No Limits

The bubbles rose up to the surface as I sank deeper into the waves. The ocean was another world. Vast. Blue. Filled with vibrant life. A school of yellow snapper swam up above, their movements in sync with the current. A few spotted eels poked their heads through some small caves, their tooth-filled mouths agape. A lobster stared at me from a ledge, shuffling along the coral.

I always felt better in the water—it was the only place where it felt like I'd never been sick, never been alone, never been in pain. Scuba diving changed everything for me.

I wasn't stuck in a hospital bed waiting for another terrible test. I wasn't going to black out anymore. I wasn't going to be in pain every time I moved. My hands weren't trembling. I didn't feel like my brain was filled with static. I was just weightless, floating in the calm water, listening to the inhale and exhale from the regulator and the bubbles climbing to the surface.

It wasn't easy getting there. I had to basically do a TED Talk for my doctor, explaining why I should go on this once-in-a-lifetime experience that my school was offering. I had to spend months weaning myself off medications that might mess with my vision and blood pressure while underwater. The hardest part was convincing my parents to let me go. I had to make a completely different presentation to them. 'If I was able to go on this trip with my friends,' I told them, 'I would be able to feel like a normal person again.' They eventually agreed, feeling better about the whole ordeal once they found out I would have to practice in a pool first in order to get my certification.

We left for our trip in April, having studied all year for our written test and practiced in pools up in Boulder. It was 5 a.m. when I met with ten other classmates at the airport. Everyone seemed half awake as they went through security, and most of us slept on the flight. I sat next to Skylar, my best friend, as she leaned against the window. She had seen me at my best and worst, never once leaving my side no matter how sick I was. She always made sure that we would have fun, even when I couldn't get out of bed. In my mind, she's like a sunflower, always looking on the bright side. Our dive trip was scheduled over her birthday, and this would be the first time she would spend it without her parents. I could tell that she was homesick already, so I made it my personal goal to make sure she was surprised with a party on the beach. My suitcase was the heaviest out of the group, Skylar having laughed at the perfect '50.0 lbs.' that had read on the scale.

"Liv, I don't think you need to pack your entire skincare routine for only five days." She smiled, tapping the side of the suitcase with her foot.

"I can't afford to get a wetsuit tan right before summer. I needed to have all the essentials!" I replied. But little did she know that half of my suitcase was filled with party streamers, gifts, hats, and even a tiny piñata for her surprise.

With only a few bumps, the plane ascended out of Denver. Like Skylar, I spent most of my time asleep or dozing off, each of us taking turns leaning on the other's shoulder. The group watched from the little windows and eventually there was water beneath us, first a deep navy shade that would eventually turn into a bright turquoise. Our eyes were glued to the sea until we landed. By the time we reached our hotel, we were tired and hungry. Room assignments went without a complaint. Skylar and I were assigned a room together, to no one's surprise. When we finally lugged our bags up to the second floor and into our room, we simply collapsed onto the beds. Unpacking would have to wait until the morning.

I've never lived on a farm or a ranch before. I don't think I would ever want to, after being abruptly awakened by a very persistent rooster. How he got onto the second-floor balcony, I don't know, but he clearly had a mission of waking everyone up right as the sun rose. I could hear the door from the boys' room open outside, one of them having the energy to shoo away the bird. I checked the clock: 6:55 a.m. I would be underwater in an hour.

After breakfast, we all boarded the dive boat with our scuba gear in hand. Skylar was my dive buddy, so we set our things across from each other. (I found time to decorate our room when I told her to go get us a table for breakfast; that way we could celebrate once we got back.) Walker, one of the tallest boys in the grade, set his stuff next to mine. He was worried about jellyfish and sharks, and our dive master quickly found joy in teasing him about it. Once everything was secured, we all went up to the bow, sitting on the edge and letting our legs hang over the side. The boat lurched as the engine came to life, and we slowly drifted out of the harbor.

Flying fish leapt up around us, following us through the waves. Turtles swam alongside the boat, their green and brown shells shining through the water. The cool spray of salt water hit our faces as we made our way to our destination.

The guides dropped anchor and we pulled on our wetsuits, laughing because it was so hard to get them adjusted. The day before we'd been reminded of the procedures that we'd be tested on — what to do if we ran out of oxygen, how to clear our masks and not panic if we needed to take them off underwater. I didn't feel frightened by any of it. I was exhilarated. Before we stepped off into the water, our instructors told us that our depth limit was sixty feet, pointing to our individual depth gauges attached to our BCDs.

But I wanted to see just how far I could go.

I was tired of limits. For years I'd struggled with a mysterious illness that had kept me from all kinds of ordinary adventures and changed my life forever. And the only reason I had gotten through it was because I wouldn't accept other people's ideas of what was possible for me. Doctors had told me I couldn't get better, and I had shown them they were wrong. I proved them wrong. I broke their limits and defied their odds. Nothing was going to stop me. Nothing could.

I checked my depth on the gauge. Exactly sixty feet.

I dove deeper.

II
Blue Dogs

I didn't realize how sick I was until I got cards sent to me from my entire class in second grade. Up until that day, I just assumed that when my classmates got sick and missed a few days of school, they were in the hospital, too. Looking back, they probably had head colds or stomach bugs, but I had always thought they were getting blood drawn or liver biopsies like I was. Or maybe they were spending the night and getting an IV. To me, this was a normal event in a little kid's life.

But we never wrote cards for those other kids when they were out of school. If the whole class had stopped everything to write to me, something must be really wrong. This was out of the ordinary. My mother laid the cards at the foot of the hospital bed for me to look through.

Skylar had drawn a picture of a pretty flower, using stickers and glitter glue. Walker had written "Get Well" with big scrawling letters. My friends Avery and Ellie had made one card for me together, showing all three of us playing soccer. Bennett, the most popular boy in the grade due to his flowy Justin Beiber hair and who all of the girls had a crush on, had made me a card with a blue dog on it. Blue was my favorite color and I loved dogs more than anything. How he knew these things was beyond my knowledge, and my mind started to race for answers. Did mini-Justin Bieber himself have a crush on me? For a moment that felt like the most wonderful, special, amazing thing in the whole world. Until my gaze fell upon the pile of get-well cards in my lap. Yeah, something was definitely wrong.

The hospital room had one small window that looked out to the gravel-filled roof of another building. My mother was sitting on the plastic hospital chair, where she had been expected to sleep for the past few nights. Through the open door I watched a nurse push a girl in a wheelchair down the hallway. She had dark circles under her eyes, her collar bones showing through her hospital gown. Her eyes were glazed over, staring at the floor as she was wheeled away. She looked like she might be dying. I wondered if I would be looking like that soon. I wondered if I might be dying, too.

I'd started blacking out just as the school year began. We'd been up in the mountains with some family friends and were about to eat dinner. I tried to sit down at the table and ended up completely missing the chair and landing on the floor. The world felt upside down and inside out. I reached out my hands as if I was balancing on a tightrope in order to steady myself, but even then, my fingers seemed to be bending and twisting.

One of the adults present, a doctor, rushed over and asked me what was going on. "Describe what you are feeling," he said as I came to. "Was it like you were spinning or was the room spinning?"

"Both," I said, rubbing my eyes to try and get rid of the feeling. The room felt warped and wobbly. My whole body was numb. "It's like when your leg falls asleep, that feeling, only everywhere."

"Have you been drinking enough water?"

Ah yes, the famous Colorado advice. "Drink more water." "The altitude is getting to you." "You must be dehydrated." I can't tell you how many doctors would tell me that was the problem in the years to come.

After that, things only got worse. A few days after second grade started, we were lining up table by table to go wash our hands before snack. I stood up when my table was called and found that I couldn't see. And this wasn't the "blurry vision" type of not seeing. It was total darkness. It felt as if I had jumped into a lake at night and opened my eyes underwater. There were no gradients or hues, just complete black that replaced my eyesight. I stood there, frozen. The only thing that kept me from completely freaking out was that the chatter of the classroom continued, and I could smell oranges and cheese sticks from the snack basket. I didn't want to cause a scene and start some rumor, so I felt around for my chair before sitting back down. I could hear the rest of my table leave, and all I could do was stare into the void that surrounded me.

"Olivia?" I heard my teacher say in a questioning manner. "Olivia." Her tone changed from curiosity to worry as her voice got closer. "Olivia!"

I flinched as something — no, someone, grabbed my shoulder. With that one touch, the abyss that I was gazing into seemed to be filled with color again, and the worried look of my teacher. The room had gone quiet, and I felt a wave of embarrassment wash over me. I pretended like nothing had happened, getting up to wash my hands at the back of the line, just as confused as the rest of the class.

Only it kept happening, and it kept getting worse. It seemed that in a matter of days, a honey-like atmosphere had engulfed my world. It felt like I was wading in it, fighting to move. I started to feel so tired, as if I was surrounded by some thick mist that I had to fight through to do anything. My back turned into a wooden board. My feet became cement blocks. My head was a foggy harbor. My blood was a roaring river of fire. My hands were cold to the touch. I quickly found comfort in the bathroom stalls, sitting on the cold tile floor and mentally preparing myself for a day of acting fine.

"Second grade is a transitional year. It can be hard for kids to adjust," said our pediatrician when we saw him. Still, he sent me for some bloodwork. But it magically came back normal. I learned a new word that day: *Hypochondriac.*

My mom begged to differ. Her motherly alarm bells were definitely going off. "There must be a virus going around," she had said originally. I figured she would fix it, like she fixed everything — another amazing superpower moms like her possessed.

Soccer practice started to become impossible. At first, I asked to be moved to defense from offense because running caused fiery pains to shoot up into my legs and spine. My shoulders would ache. It hurt when I turned my head to watch the ball. A lot of my friends moved up to more competitive teams, but I couldn't find the energy to continue with them.

I wasn't a big reader before second grade, but the moment I quit soccer I started to find myself reading books to pass the time. Reading was a lot like scuba diving, allowing me to ignore my symptoms and become lost in another world. At first, I started with the typical second grade books like *Geronimo Stilton* and *The Magic Tree House*. But since I now had the time, my reading quickly became more advanced as I started reading the *Harry Potter* and *Maze Runner* series. However, the series that I became most passionate about was *Percy Jackson and the Olympians*. I didn't share much in common with British wizards, but I easily found myself in Rick Riordan's characters. The idea that conditions like ADHD and dyslexia were early signs of being a powerful demigod was something I could totally relate to through my own symptoms, and by the time I was twelve, part of me was hoping a satyr might show up at my door.

My first surgery was the removal of my adenoids, which my doctor suspected could be the issue. When I woke up, I was handed a red slushie and told that hopefully this would be the end of my symptoms. Drinking the slushie felt like chugging a cup of glass shards, but they told me that was a normal reaction and not a new symptom I had gotten. I expected to be fine by the next few days, but when I still felt awful after a week, I knew the surgery did nothing except make me snore less. A few weeks later, I noticed that my hands would not stop shaking. It got so bad that holding a pencil or trying to type was a challenge. At one point I tried to teach myself how to get prettier handwriting, but even now my writing shows how bad the tremor could get.

I practiced how to keep my balance in case I lost my vision at school. I taught myself to stand with my legs crossed, knees pressing into each other and feet perpendicular. I would rather have kids ask me if I did ballet instead of asking me why I fell over in the middle of class.

My school held a choir concert one night, and I was on the top row with the rest of the taller kids. The whole student body was there, and I started to feel like I was about to collapse. I swayed back and forth, my vision going in and out of focus. I made eye contact with Ms. Rhodes, who was standing on the side of the stage. In a few moments, my choir teacher walked up to the side of the bleachers, grabbing my hand and walking me down to the front row. I was now even more nervous to fall face flat in front of the crowd. At least on the top row I could maybe fall backwards into the curtain like some fancy stunt. Surprisingly, the performance ended with me still on my feet. And as the other parents were wondering what had happened, my parents rushed me out of the school and sped towards the emergency room.

I was tested for nearly everything. I lost track of how much blood they took. Doctors I didn't know bustled in and out of the room. I had x-rays, EKGs, and endoscopies. I was still frightened of needles in those days so they would only put in IVs at night. My mom usually stayed with me, and my dad was at home with my little twin brothers.

One night, however, there was a test that required me to stay up to at least midnight. My dad offered to stay up with me, and we ended up watching *The Croods* twice before I was finally allowed to sleep. Apparently, someone took a photo of me that night when I was hooked up to wires and monitors. I didn't notice until the fourth grade, when our class got laptops for the first time, and we all decided to look up our names on the internet. I was mortified when someone showed me that photo.

I just wanted to be normal like the other kids.

I wanted to go home.

One afternoon I had an MRI. It's kind of ironic how you go into this machine and they tell you it's completely safe and then all of the technicians step behind a glass wall to protect themselves. But they did let me bring in my stuffed dog, Maxine. She's a little black lab plush and she's been through everything with me. I'd sleep with her every night, clutched so tightly in my arm that she lost most of the stuffing in her middle. My grandmother, whom I call Bebe, sewed her up for me so many times. She tried to bring her actual dog, Rosie, to be with me in the hospital, saying it was an emotional support animal, but they didn't buy it.

During the day, my parents put on a brave face, but at night, when they thought I was asleep, I could always hear their hushed, worried voices. My mother was getting more frustrated by the minute, and one night I could even hear my dad cry. It was the first time in my life where I had witnessed him do that, and it scared me far beyond the IVs, MRIs, and blood draws.

One day, after countless tests and nurses cycled through my room, one doctor finally stopped to talk to us. He announced that I tested negative for Wilson's Disease, as if I already knew what that was.

"Really?" my mother gasped. "Oh, thank goodness."

I still had no idea what was going on, but her sudden burst of relief made me worried. "Mom, am I going to die?"

"No!" she assured me.

It turned out that some of the doctors thought I might have this very rare disease, an inability to process copper in your body, and that I'd be dead before I turned forty. I hadn't even known it at the time, but my mom had been doing tons of research and already found the very best hospital for Wilson's which coincidentally was at the University of Michigan, where a family friend worked alongside the top scientists for the illness. The major diagnosis for Wilson's Disease was a genetic test, which had just come back negative. Everyone was celebrating the good news.

I wasn't. I was still feeling miserable in the hospital bed. It dawned on me that the countless doctors I had seen had yet to figure out what was wrong. Maybe I had another rare disease that was going to kill me.

"So did you guys *find* anything?" I asked in a small voice.

"Well," said the doctor, turning serious again. "The atmosphere in Colorado is very dry. When you live at altitude you really do have to drink a lot of water."

Wow. Just a few minutes ago they thought I was going to die and now they were telling me I was just dehydrated?

My mother was shaking her head. "Are you guys serious? This is what the smartest doctors in Colorado can come up with? Drink more water? That's obviously not the problem because you've been giving her so many fluids already. We need a real answer!"

But none of the doctors who saw me could figure out the problem. Over the next year I would go to over fifty different specialists. They ordered tests and more tests. They studied the results and passed us along to other specialists. Sometimes I would get a new doctor, never see him once, and then be told by a nurse that he gave up and passed me on to someone else.

When they discharged me from the hospital, they insisted that I sit in a wheelchair. But I didn't want to. I wanted to walk. I wanted to run. I wanted to play soccer again.

The day I returned to Ms. Rhodes's classroom I saw a list on the chalkboard: "Things Olivia Likes for Her Card." The color blue was the first thing on the list. Dogs was the second. Bennett, swishing his hair at his desk like a celebrity, didn't even notice me come back to the room. He'd just drawn a blue dog because the teacher told him to. I took a seat, trying to hold my head up. Not because I was sad - okay, maybe a little bit - but recently my neck had been hurting so much that I had to physically try to keep my head from lolling to the side. I looked straight ahead, trying not to pay attention to how many kids were staring at me and whispering.

There, written on the bulletin board above that dumb list were three words that had been there since the first day of school: *Imagine. Wonder. Dream.*

"What do those mean?" asked a girl at the beginning of the year.

"Well, if you do all of that," Ms. Rhodes said, "it means anything is possible."

I looked at them now. *Imagine. Wonder. Dream.* Okay, I thought, that's what I'm going to have to do.

Dear Parents,

As kids, we tend to put the blame on ourselves when we see you stressed out. My mom was a theater major, studying facial expressions and body language. But even though she is a professional, I can still tell when she is worried. Even if she looks fine, her voice tends to raise an octave higher, especially when I was in the hospital. She wasn't okay—and it was because I was sick.

Kids hide how they are feeling because they don't want to make their parents worry. I would have gotten pretty far hiding my symptoms if it wasn't for my teachers watching over me and noticing how awful I looked and felt. I wanted my parents to be proud of me for excelling at school, not anxious about me being absent and sick. When the doctors would wonder if I was making it up, a part of me would say, 'well, yes, I am technically lying about feeling good'. But looking back, lying about how I felt could have been one of the many reasons why my disease became chronic, and why I still have it now. If I had told them sooner, maybe I would have gotten diagnosed earlier. But my eight-year-old self couldn't let my parents worry about me and my health. And that's exactly what ended up happening.

We know you are missing work, missing friends, spending a lot of money, and neglecting your own health to take care of us, and we feel terrible about it. When we are chronically sick, we start feeling like a burden on those we love. It happens all the time.

So, as parents, what can you do about that?

Know that we see every detail of what you are doing—making appointments, researching on the internet, keeping lists of all of our medications, talking to our teachers. All on top of your regular parental duties like grocery shopping, laundry, making meals, and taking us to school. When you're really sick, you get used to noticing everything around you. You don't have the luxury of being distracted by friends or sports.

The illness is like an invader, an enemy, and it can drive you apart from each other as a family—or it can bring you together. But it's going to take teamwork from everyone.

Try not to get angry at your kid. Try not to be frustrated that they aren't getting better or that the medicine isn't working. We tend to think that we are failing you. Don't make it worse. Most of all, Mom and Dad, don't ever fight about what's going on in front of your child. Everyone needs to be a united front. If you guys don't agree about the doctor's approach or the diagnosis or the next right steps, have those arguments in private. Because I assure you that if you do it in front of us, we are going to feel responsible for how you are doing as a couple on top of everything else.

Be curious. Don't just ask how we are doing, but instead encourage us to open up and really talk about everything that's going on. Don't try to fix things too fast and be comfortable with what a hard time we are having. Don't let our hard time be your hard time. I mean, it is, but try to realize that the illness is the problem, not us.

And be persistent. If my parents weren't persistent, I wouldn't be here. They believed me, even when the doctors told them it was all in my head. They believed me when I said I was sick, and they believed that I was going to get better. And their faith in me and my experience is why I am doing so well.

You are going to get through this as a family. And you just might find yourselves a lot closer than before. We did. And that was one of the greatest gifts we got from this journey.

Have hope and be brave,

Olivia

III

Fearless

In first grade at the National Western Stock Show, I was one of the Mutton Busters. It's safe to say that I was a fearless little kid.

Mutton Busting is where you, a seven-year-old, climb onto a sheep twice your size, and when they open the gate there is only one goal: hold on for dear life as you get rushed across the stadium. The crowd would cheer as the sheep tried to buck you off, running in circles, zig zags, and even into the walls. I saw kids get dragged in the dirt, bucked off, and trampled. And whichever kid had the stamina to hold on the longest would win. We wore helmets, as if that would save us from a storm of hooves. It was wild and reckless, and I absolutely loved it.

My dad practiced with me at home. He got on his hands and knees in the living room, and I climbed onto his back and then he pretended to be a grumpy sheep. I'd hold on tight with my arms and my legs. "Baaaa!" exclaimed my dad, laughing. Jack and Will, my little brothers, ran around us trying to distract me. But I was deeply focused on my incentive training.

My mom knew I was going to be the only girl on the Mutton Busting team and she was determined that everyone would know that. "With that helmet on, they'll just think you are another little boy," she told me. "So we are curling your hair and dressing you in all pink. I know you prefer blue, but this way everyone will know that you're a strong young lady."

On the big day at the actual rodeo, I got a sheep with a white coat and an all-black face except for a raindrop of white on his snout. He was the only black sheep in the flock. The moment I clambered onto his back, though, he began to paw the dirt with his hoof, already wanting me off. I dug my hands into the rough wool on his back. I immediately felt like I might fall off. A bell rang, the gate clicked open, and all the sheep took off.

I was sliding from side to side. The boy before me slipped off his sheep who stepped on him. I could hear him howling in pain from the stands. I buried my face into the sheep's back, determined not to let go. I knew my parents were in the audience, but the cheers were just a dull background hum. The sheep was making irritable grunting noises. He wanted me off.

I love animals so much. I kept convincing my grandmother and my parents to get just one more dog, which is the reason why we now collectively have five dogs between the two houses. I dreamt about growing up and being a vet or working at an animal shelter. I had two huge drawers filled with stuffed animals and I would pretend to give them stitches and take care of them. Once, our family had swum with dolphins on a vacation and I had fallen in love with a rescued dolphin called Alex, who was a real troublemaker. When he whistled and clicked you could tell he was sassing back at the instructors at the aquarium. By far the best attitude I have ever seen in an animal.

The sheep that I was on also had an attitude, but I could take him. I concentrated as hard as I could. I held on as hard as I could. I was flopping from side to side. The sheep arched his back and bolted. Boom! I was off—and in the mud. My pretty pink outfit was covered in dirt, but I had held on the longest.

My parents were running over to congratulate me. I got a giant trophy that was taller than me. I couldn't even lift it and my dad had to carry it home.

Bad things just didn't happen to me then. I didn't get sick. I never had accidents. My little brothers were always needing stitches for having busted open their foreheads or getting casts for broken arms. Not me.

I was on a soccer team called the Cheetah Girls, and I was one of the fastest runners. Avery, Ellie, and I would all chase after the ball together, laughing. I loved bungee jumping, riding the biggest roller coasters, and rock climbing. I'd always be the first one to the top.

When we would go alpine sledding, I always went zipping down in the fast lane. I'd see people who'd taken curves too fast and flipped off their sleds and crashed, but I never did. I figured it was their fault. They must have done something wrong. But me? I was fine and I didn't worry about anything.

Avery was my best friend in those days. Our mothers were best friends, too, and at the end of each school day we'd just get into my car or her mom's car, whoever was picking us up. We spent the night at each other's houses. My dad, who coached our soccer team, always put us on opposite sides during practices so we wouldn't distract each other. But then we didn't care who won. If Avery's team won, it was the same as if my team did. We were that close. We went to the same camps. We did after-school cooking and art programs together. But the teachers kept us apart at school. They knew not to put us in the same class unless they wanted chaos.

There was this one place between our two houses at Robinson Park where only the brave kids went. There were trees to climb and a playground with swings and a jungle gym, but we went up the hill to this long green maze of thick bushes. Kids said foxes lived in there, and there were often broken bottles littered around the ground. We'd frequently see a lot of teenagers sneak in during the summer.

The challenge was to climb in through this tiny opening in the thick mesh of prickly branches and tunnel through to the other side without getting lost or trapped. Avery's older brother had done it and we wanted to do it, too.

"You nervous?" Avery asked me the day we finally decided to take the dare.

I shook my head. I wasn't. I did feel butterflies in my stomach, but I liked that feeling of being on the edge of something new. I liked adventure. This was a quest, one that I was going to fulfill.

I really wanted to be able to say that we'd done it, we'd made it through. That would be enough too.

We crouched down in the dirt and tried not to touch the old wrappers and dirty socks lying around. The prickles caught on our hair and we helped each other get untangled so we could get inside the labyrinth.

"Maybe we shouldn't do this," Avery worried.

"C'mon," I urged her. "This way."

All the leaves kept out the sun and it was dark inside the hedge. The ground was packed down and hard. Far away we could hear the voices of the kids in the playground but there was an eerie silence all around us. I could hear my heart beating. The single path branched off into other dense areas, leaving us in the middle.

Ahead of me I could see a small patch of sunlight and I scrambled forward, branches scratching across my back. Avery followed behind me. We were finally out.

We stood up and, with a groan, realized we were right in the middle of the thicket. We had to get down in the dirt again and wiggle through the prickly branches some more. We had a lot further to go. But by now we were used to it. We had smudges of mud across our cheeks, little bits of this and that in our hair. The tunnel we were following branched off again.

"Which way do we go?" wondered Avery. "Maybe we should turn around. What if we get stuck in here and we never find our way out?"

"We'll circle back if we need to. C'mon, we can do this!"

Finally, up ahead we could see little patches of bright green. Grass. Sunlight. This time we really were on the other side. We clambered out, dusty and dirty. We stood up, triumphant. Avery was beaming, twigs sticking out of her hair and dirt on her nose.

Sometimes, in the years to come, I would remember that afternoon journey. While all the other kids were swinging or throwing balls back and forth, we were going into the darkness. There was no clear path. No signs to tell us which way to go. And just when we thought it was all over, we discovered we were only in the middle—nowhere close to the end. But we kept on going, and that's what mattered.

From my bedroom window I could look out over Robinson Park. In the years to come, I would watch kids in the playground, eating popsicles in the summer or sledding in the winter. And I would rarely leave my room anymore, too sick to join them. I would gaze at the dark hedge on the farthest side of the park, remembering that I was able to make it through.

IV
Fireflies

Every summer since my grandmother was nine years old, my family and I would go to the Lake of the Ozarks. People wondered why we would rather be in a landlocked state in the middle of the country and not at some beach. The truth is that the lake is a hidden gem, and no one knows about it. It's also a huge family tradition and all of my family meets down there in July.

That summer after my miserable year in second grade, I was so relieved to be there. I walked in the house, down to the basement, and up to a plastic fish on a plaque, titled 'Billy the Bass Fish'. I pressed a tiny red button, and the fish sprung to life, opening its mouth and singing,

"Here's a little song I wrote,

You might want to sing it note for note,

Don't worry, be happy."

I put on my life jacket and headed down to the lake. When I floated in the water, the pain disappeared for a little while. The worry disappeared, too. Later on, in our boat, I'd listen to the water slapping against the hull, feeling more relaxed than ever.

We loved to take our boat to our favorite barbecue restaurant with the best onion rings I've ever had. At the end of every meal on the lake, people throw their French fries into the water and huge carp and catfish swim up to eat them. Once, my brother Jack said he wanted to hang upside down to feed the fish and my dad flipped him right over into the water, and we all laughed. Jack never asked to do that again.

At night we loved to catch fireflies all around our house. We'd run around outside trying to cup them in our hands. One time, Jack somehow got a firefly in his eye, and the entire side of his face started to glow. *Plink... plink... plink.* We were trying not to laugh while he freaked out. He rubbed his eye, and it flew out and away as fast as it could.

Later the doctors would ask me, "Did you go into the woods? How long were you in the woods?"

But I didn't. The branches of the huge oak trees hung over our road, but we never left the buckled pavement. We never went into the woods. There were spiders, snakes, and poison ivy everywhere.

Sometimes after my brothers went to bed, my mom and I would go outside, walking up and down the driveway to try and catch fireflies. She would always tell me not to go into the woods or else I would touch poison ivy. With firefly-filled mason jars in our hands, we would hear cicadas chirp while soft waves hit the dock. It was peaceful, serene. The calm before the storm. How could this possibly have been the time when I was in the greatest danger?

I mean, there are plenty of bugs in the Ozarks. You wake up in the morning and the screens are black with little mosquitos. Swarms of June bugs click and whir against the windows. Spiders the size of your hand hide under boat lifts. The one kind of bug we never saw out at the lake was ticks. We didn't even see them on our dogs, who were out in the forest all the time. The fact that we couldn't see them is what makes them so dangerous.

V
Burning

I finally got diagnosed with Lyme disease when I was in third grade. At this point I was lying on the floor because my neck muscles kept giving out.

My mom was so angry at our pediatrician and demanded that he find someone to help us figure out what was going on. There had to be someone in this state who could come up with an answer, right?

Right before Christmas I was introduced to Dr. Lafayette, an incredibly nice woman who immediately ordered tests the moment she saw me. It had gotten worse around the time I saw her, as if I had three cases of the flu stacked on top of each other. At that point I was sick of doctors' visits and tests, wanting nothing more than to sleep the holidays away.

But in January Dr. Lafayette called us back. "I know why you haven't been feeling good," she announced confidently. "You have Lyme disease."

I didn't even know what that was.

"Isn't that an East Coast thing?" asked my mom, confused.

"It's everywhere, technically. Do you remember getting bit by a tick?"

Both my mom and I shook our heads.

"Well, you were. Your western blot was positive. You've got it. But here's the really good news. One month of antibiotics and you'll be better! You can start today!"

I'd gone from having a mysterious illness that might kill me to a pill every morning for thirty days. After five days I felt better already. Good as new. Starting up soccer again was the only thing on my mind as a realized I could now do everything I had missed out on.

My mom and dad were so relieved. "Our kid is finally back! She's got her sparkle again."

But just a few days after I finished the antibiotics, I was worse than ever. Every single part of my body hurt. I felt like I was probably dying, but I was too tired to even care.

Everybody has times in their lives when they look back and think, "What if?" What if Dr. Lafayette had known exactly how to treat me? What if she had given me antibiotics for six weeks instead of four? That might have made all the difference. But that's not what happened.

Unfortunately, there weren't a lot of doctors who treated Lyme disease in Colorado. And Dr. Lafayette wasn't an expert. But my mother found Dr. K, who had some experience with tick-borne illnesses, and we went to see this wacky guy who had an office in his basement. Looking back, that was probably the first of many red flags. You weren't allowed to wear perfume and you had to take your shoes off before you came inside, but he promised he knew how to make me better.

Or at least that's what he said in the beginning.

He gave me drugs and herbs and supplements and none of them made much of a difference. I would often end up taking all of them in the morning, going to school, throwing them all up before lunch, and going home to do it all over again.

We went to him for almost two years. We didn't want to give up. I mean, we knew what was wrong with me. Why wasn't I getting better? I missed birthday parties. I missed school trips. I'd lie on the couch and watch my friends riding their bikes up and down the street, too sick to get up. Nobody knew how hard I was working just to get out of bed every morning. They had no idea that I spent nearly half an hour each morning mentally encouraging myself, and then another ten minutes literally trying to sit up and stand.

I was really starting to feel hopeless. One day at one of our appointments I asked the question I was most scared about. "Dr. K, are we going to get this Lyme disease out of my body or am I going to be sick for the rest of my life?"

He barely even paused. He didn't make eye contact with me. "Olivia, you are going to have this for the rest of your life. If it had been found sooner and treated properly, you might have gotten better but now you are going to have to live with it."

Live with it? I was barely living. Was that all this doctor could do? Keep me from dying? I couldn't breathe. I tried to keep it together but by the time we got to the car, hot tears were streaming down my face.

My mother was gripping the steering wheel and staring straight ahead. I could almost see steam coming out of her ears. I'd never seen her so angry. "We are going to figure this out," she said at last. "You are going to get better. I know it. All he did was tell us that he's not a very good doctor. That's his problem. It's not ours anymore. If we have to fly to the moon and go find treatment up there, we'll do it. If we have to go to the Amazon River, or Mount Everest, we'll do it. I will not stop until you are better. Olivia, that is my promise to you."

On the way home I stared out the window at the sky. Why couldn't I have some disease that people knew how to treat? If I had diabetes, the doctors would know what to do. If I had cancer, they would at least *know* something.

My mother reached out to touch my arm reassuringly, but her touch burned like her hands were made of fire. "You cannot touch my skin," I yelped. "My skin is on fire. Everything is burning."

Wasn't there anyone who could put out the fire?

Dear Doctors,

It's not our fault we are sick. It's not our fault that what's making us sick is complicated or mysterious. It's not our fault that you can't figure out what's going on and what to do to make us better.

I saw over fifty doctors before I was correctly diagnosed and most of them are a blur of white coats staring at their computer screens. I don't remember their faces or their names, just that they'd order a bunch of tests and then get frustrated and tell me I probably needed to see someone else. Or they told me that it was all in my head. They implied that I was passing out to get attention, that I liked being stuck at home lying in bed all day, that I wanted to be sick. Sometimes I wonder if this is what they did with all of their difficult cases. Did they always make it seem like it was our fault—because even with all of their training and expertise they were stumped?

How many people actually make up their symptoms? Not that many. It's not common. Let me tell you that I would have much rather been healthy than sick. And that a lot of these doctors who acted like I was a hypochondriac made me feel hopeless and crazy on top of everything else. I began to think I'd be sick for the rest of my life and no one would ever believe me.

The difference, finally, between a good doctor and a bad doctor for me is that the good ones didn't give up. They could admit when they were confused but they were persistent. They asked me how I was doing and after that, they actually listened to my answers. I wasn't just a body in a hospital bed to them. I was a person who needed help.

If I have any advice for doctors, it would be, "Don't give up on your patients. If the test comes back and doesn't make any sense, do a different test. If the medicine doesn't work, research a different medicine. Call up someone and ask for help. Follow up with your patients even when you send them to another specialist. If you can't figure out what's wrong, don't feel like you are doing a bad job. This is the time to be Sherlock Holmes or Dr. House. Treat the illness as a challenge or a quest, not a problem."

The truth is that my Lyme disease was obvious to everyone who did the right tests. Now, the first doctor who diagnosed me had never even seen a case of Lyme disease, but she followed a hunch and ordered the right test. She thought about things. She was persistent and thorough about diagnosing me and for that I am grateful. Now she was just following what the CDC suggested on their website when it came to treatment, and she had no idea how inadequate the suggestions were at that time, but at least she tried to help me get better.

But all of those earlier doctors? I feel like they wasted their education and training by giving up on me so easily. What does that say about our whole medical system if doctors don't trust their patients? What does it say if they can't work out difficult cases? What does it mean if so many of them can't diagnose an obvious case of an illness that is running rampant in our country?

Pay attention to the details. Don't just look at the test results. Look at the patient's whole record. Look at the patient. Ask questions. Real questions. Remember that the patient is a real person and you are a real person. So many of the doctors I saw were like faceless mannequins. They didn't let me know who they were and they didn't know who I was. It was a nightmare. Really.

I'm just asking you to believe your patients. And believe in yourself. Believe that you can figure out what's the matter. Believe that you can be a real healer and make a difference in someone's life.

Is that too much to ask? I don't think so.

Olivia

VI
Limes

When Avery and I got together, we made plans. We made plans for the babysitting business we were going to start when we were old enough. We got ready making the posters and flyers we would post around the neighborhood. We imagined all the money we were going to make—and the mansions, right next door to each other, that we were going to buy. We planned for the dogs we were going to get. Avery's dream dog was a husky named Shasta and I wanted a Doberman named Cerberus. Most of all, we were both going to have daughters, and they were going to become best friends just like us.

We talked about everything—soccer, school, camp, and how stupid it was that Katy Perry's music video for "Dark Horse" was set in Egypt when the song literally mentioned Aphrodite.

"All I'm saying is that it's wrong," I explained to Avery. "She's a Greek goddess and that whole set was Egyptian."

"You're like Hermione, but for mythology," laughed Avery. "But yeah, I agree. It was stupid."

Still, we loved Katy Perry and watched her all the time along with dog videos, lots of funny dog videos, and laughed together.

The one thing I didn't tell Avery was about my last visit with Dr. K., and how he was keeping me alive but not making me *feel* alive. I didn't tell her that he said that I was never going to get better and that I was going to be sick with Lyme for the rest of my life.

Because I wasn't.

Dr. K. was wrong. I was going to get better no matter what he said.

By the time my mom and I had pulled into the driveway after our last trip to him, I had stopped crying and I was ready to make a plan.

"What about those boys we read about who went to Germany?" I asked my mom. We'd heard on the internet about these kids who couldn't walk or read—and then they went abroad for this special new Lyme treatment and they were feeling completely better.

My mom's face fell. "I didn't want to tell you. They're sick again. Worse than ever."

"But someone might invent a cure, right?" I asked. "Like with ALS. It doesn't have a cure now but that doesn't mean there's not one out there. We did the Ice Bucket Challenge to help spread awareness and now since enough people know about it, they have more funding, right?"

I had seen all the viral videos of the challenge sweep the internet. Even celebrities were participating and donating to help ALS research.

"I wonder if there's anything like that with Lyme," I asked out loud.

And just like that, my mom was on it.

It was almost perfect how it just happened to be May at the time. We discovered that May was officially Lyme Disease Awareness month, and they did in fact have a challenge already. Together, my mom and I watched some of the Lyme challenge videos online.

"All you have to do is videotape yourself eating a lime?" I said, reading the description of the challenge. "How hard is that?"

"Have you ever sucked on a lime?" My mom laughed, her face puckering at the thought of it.

Avery and I set up lemonade stands all the time, which was another one of our favorite summer get-rich plans. If we could cut up a bag of lemons, we could cut up a few limes and eat them. I got on the phone with her right away.

"Let's do it tomorrow!" said Avery. "I'll come right over after breakfast."

There was so much to plan! Who were we going to call out and challenge? What were we going to wear? Would this really make a difference?

"We need to invite Calvin and Skylar and Walker," I said, making a list.

"Don't forget Emily and Lucile and Lucas," added Avery. "They'll do it for sure. Our video is going to be amazing!"

"Definitely better than Katy Perry's video!"

"No pyramids!" giggled Avery.

The sun was shining the next day, perfect for shooting our video in the backyard. My mom was going to do the filming, but she had to get the limes first.

Avery and I played Minecraft while we waited. We had so many worlds together and they were all filled with dogs, probably too many. I was the miner and builder, and she was the flower picker and interior designer.

As soon as my mom got back, we cut up our limes and headed into the backyard. We had our lists of friends and family to challenge, but we hadn't figured out how to pronounce all of the last names.

"Stepanock . . ." I began.

"Stefanock . . ." corrected Avery.

"Stefanopoulos . . ." said my mom. "And don't hold your notes in front of your faces!"

We needed a lot of takes to get it right. Turns out making a video is not as easy as it seems. But the one thing we only had to film once was taking a bite out of our limes.

"One . . . two . . . three!"

We opened our mouths wide and sucked on our slices of lime.

My whole face squiggled shut. Avery stuck out her tongue. We shut our eyes, wincing at the bitter, sour taste.

You can see it on the video, my original lime face. There I am, all puckered up.

Now when I eat a lime, I barely even notice it. It's just another lime. I've eaten so many limes over the years they taste sweet to me at this point. I've probably eaten a whole tree of them. Wherever I go, people want to video themselves eating a lime with me, and I have to fake my sour face.

I had no plan for what was about to happen. Avery and I posted the video to Facebook and Instagram and waited to see if any of our friends would like it.

"Elise likes it!"

"Oh my God! Luke liked it!"

"We got ten likes, Avery, that's huge!"

"We just got another one, that's eleven. We got eleven likes! We're famous!"

"You know what?" I decided on the spot. "We are doing this at school and I'm going to challenge all kinds of people like . . ." I tried to think of someone famous who might actually do it. "I got it! Governor Hickenlooper! We'll get the Governor of Colorado to do the Lyme Challenge and then it will go really big and some scientist will hear about it and get to work and there will be a cure for Lyme disease. We are going to make it happen, right?"

"It's a plan!" grinned Avery.

My mom was smiling at us. "This is amazing, girls. But do remember that people like Governor Hickenlooper are awfully busy. They get a lot of requests like this."

"We can ask, can't we?" I said.

"Of course you can. Dream big," answered my mom.

So Avery and I brought a bag of limes to school and got everyone in our advisory to take a bite out of a lime. Our teacher suggested someone write an article about it for the school newspaper, but we never expected what happened next. A local reporter heard about the Lyme Challenge and put us in *The Denver Post*.

And even Governor Hickenlooper heard about it through my letter I sent him and invited me to the capitol building to take the Lyme Challenge with him.

Eventually I'd take the Lyme Challenge with the band members of Imagine Dragons and the cast of *Modern Family*. Mark Hamill, aka *the* Luke Skywalker from *Star Wars*, would do the Lyme Challenge when I called him out. All kinds of senators and congress people around the country would take a bite out of a lime. Eventually I'd even be invited to be a junior ambassador for the Lyme Challenge.

Avery and I could never have imagined it would all go so big that day in my backyard.

Twelve likes became a thousand shares and ten thousand followers.

But Avery wouldn't be one of them.

Maybe she began to feel left out. Maybe she was jealous or competitive. I don't really know. One day I texted her and she never texted me back. She ghosted me.

She stopped coming over, she pretended she didn't know me, she never looked at me in the halls again. And I still don't know why.

That wasn't part of our plan. But that's one of the hardest things I've learned since I've been sick. It's really hard to know what's going to happen next.

VII
Contagious

A lot of people tend to have some pretty rough middle school experiences. I was one of them, which isn't much of a surprise. Not even a week of being a middle schooler and I already had someone trying to ruin the year for me. Her name was Kelly, and she's the reason why the entire school thought I was contagious.

"So Olivia," she happily announced in a stage whisper. "You have a disease, right?"

Kids swiveled around in their chairs and stared at me. Our teacher Mrs. Williamson kept on writing on the board like nothing was happening.

"Yeah." I shrugged, trying not to make it a big deal. After all, I'd given a big talk about Lyme disease to my whole grade the year before. Everyone should know what it was by now. What was her point?

Kelly smirked. "And diseases are contagious, right?" She practically hissed the word.

"Not all of them are. Not mine," I answered evenly.

"Are you sure?" she asked, in the tone one would use when talking to a toddler. A group of girls, her friends, giggled behind us.

"Yes, I'm positive." I looked back down at my paper. My feet hurt. My joints ached. I felt like I was going to pass out. It was hard enough to get through the day without this. On my way to lunch a little later I heard another group of girls giggling as I passed. I noticed that Avery was amongst them.

"You shouldn't be here," they whispered. Great.

Of course, the cafeteria had to be overly crowded that day. "Oh, I'm sorry this table's full. You can't sit here, anyways." Kelly picked up an apple core, waving it in the air before setting it down on the open chair.

Finally, I sat down at a table on the other end of the room. Millie, a class-mate, was just about to sit down with me when, of course, Kelly had to show up. "You don't want to sit with her. She's sick and she'll get you sick too."

Millie believed her and left.

In middle school everyone wanted to be part of a group. They wanted to be one of the cool girls in 'The Squad' (it's what they liked to call themselves) or the popular girls who all planned their matching outfits each day. They all wanted to belong. They all wanted to fit in, and how they made themselves worthy was by spreading rumors. About me.

The one person I could really count on was Skylar, and Kelly hated that. Kelly did everything in her power to get rid of that bond. She made Skylar listen to her speaking in Pig Latin, trying to teach her that way they could have private conversations in front of me. Skylar refused to learn, and I guess Kelly never realized I could understand her the entire time.

"Hey, I get it. I get you want to exclude me," I confronted Kelly in the hallway, making sure my tone was casual and uncaring. "But don't talk about me in a different language when I'm right there. Skylar can't even understand you. She doesn't want to understand you."

Kelly gave me this cold stare before turning her gaze to Skylar. "Is that true, Skylar?"

Skylar wasn't one to stand up for herself. Part of me thought she wouldn't answer or would just agree with Kelly to avoid conflict. However, Skylar looked at me before saying, "Yeah, it's kind of true."

With a huff of annoyance, Kelly returned her focus to me. "What's the matter with you?" Kelly shouted, red splotches appearing on her neck. "You know what? If you keep *bullying* me, I'm gonna leave the school!"

I looked down at her. "I am perfectly fine with that."

I knew it was all talk. I would love it if she left but her parents had sunk too much money into the school to leave at this point. And she didn't seem like the kind of kid to take no for an answer.

For the next few years, she would devote herself to making me seem like the mean one. She would try to trip me while walking to class or shove me while attempting to play soccer again at recess. When I told her to stop, she would plaster a cheeky smile on her face and say, "I think your disease is making you crazy. I didn't do any of that."

She would tell the teachers I was faking it. "But she looks fine!" she would always start out when I was about to leave for the nurse's office. "Mrs. Williamson, Olivia was perfectly okay at lunch. I don't see why she has to go to the nurse right now. I think she just wants to get out of PE."

"What's going on, Olivia? Is that true?" asked the teacher in front of everyone.

For the thousandth time I had to explain how my symptoms came and went. That one moment I'd be dizzy and the next moment I couldn't see, and then it would pass. I still made it my priority to hide my symptoms, so Kelly's accusations almost gave me a pat on the back for my acting skills. I knew she would see me race out of the class when the lunch bell rang, only to lean against the lockers to try and not pass out in front of the grade. I would pretend to open up my locker, shaky fingers spinning the lock in random directions. Either I was actually convincing her I was fine, or she didn't care if I wasn't. Probably the latter. Mrs. Williamson never did anything about the bullying. "Talk it out, ladies," she would say before walking away.

Anytime I would go up to Kelly to confront her, she'd call her group of look-alikes, using them as social shields. She would say something, maybe call me a wuss or a crybaby, and then her clones would echo it. Imagine the seagulls from *Finding Nemo*. That's them, except they had matching pink bracelets and cat ear headbands.

My work started magically disappearing from my art class. Just before they were finished, paintings, sculptures, and drawings would seemingly vanish from the classroom drawer. I would be the only kid without anything on the wall for my school's annual art show. Just before I graduated, my art teacher finally found all of my pieces hidden in a pile behind a ceramics shelf, which was in a completely different building. Some were drawn on with red pen, and others were torn up or smashed. The teacher called my mom, furious. "I know exactly who did this. And I want you to know that they are the meanest group of girls I have seen in all my years of teaching."

The real disease in our school was bullying. And rumors were the most contagious of them all.

There were some teachers who were just mean to everyone and didn't care what was going on. There were teachers who let me keep my medicine in their desks and asked how I was feeling, but never noticed how much I was being bullied. There were teachers who were good at comforting me. But none of them solved anything.

Not until Mr. McWell.

The kids bullied him, too. He was tall and loud and everyone made fun of it. One day in class, a boy, being a typical middle school boy, flushed another kid's sneaker down the toilet. Mr. McWell was the first to know about it, and instead of keeping things discreet, he casually called the boy out in front of the class, calling him a "dickhead". Probably not the best teaching moment, but no one made fun of Mr. McWell after that.

He never let me walk to the nurse by myself, which was new. He'd asked me about my symptoms at the end of each day and when they were happening, almost as if he was learning how to spot them. No one dared to make fun of me when he was around. He even brought in pillows so I could lay down on the desk when my head became too heavy to carry. He knew I wasn't faking it. My eighth-grade math teacher was also one of the rare teachers who had truly supported me. And it turned out she used to be a drag racer in Jamaica.

"Donovan, are you messing with Olivia?"

"No," he answered, embarrassed at being called by his full name.

"That's what I thought," she said firmly.

She knew how to keep an eye on everyone and everything and stop the bullying at the get-go.

I developed a kind of immunity to bullying after years of experiencing it. I learned how to deflect it and make the taunting conversations short. All I had to do was baffle them with my responses.

"I hate you Olivia," some kid I barely knew told me.

"Really? Wow, that's crazy. I hate me too," I answered blandly. I'd learned how to defuse the situation.

All of a sudden his face changed, as if he'd been snapped out of a trance. "Wait, what? No, I'm sorry, that's terrible. I didn't mean that."

Looking back on it, I realized that I was preparing myself to be in the public eye and learning how to deflect negative opinions on who I was and what I was trying to accomplish. When I became an advocate for Lyme disease, people would say that I was faking it for fame. When I spoke at conferences, people would accuse my parents of exploiting me. But I'd learned not to care what other people thought. I couldn't let myself become attached to those parasitic rumors. I had to remain true to myself.

I learned to keep my true friends close—Skylar, Amelia, Lucas, and Walker. I didn't need a big group to hang around with. I needed friends I could trust. I didn't need followers who would agree with every word I said. By the end of middle school, the groups of mean girls were fighting with each other, and I was finally at peace with my own friends.

Dear Classmates,

There's probably a kid in your class right now who seems to be a little bit different from the rest. Maybe they're shy, or don't hang out with your friend group. In most cases, these kinds of people tend to have a lot going on outside of school. They mean well but might not have the energy to show it. They're often the prime targets for bullying. So instead of watching them get knocked down or harassed by students, maybe try to stand up for them, or ask them to hang out with you instead. They'll appreciate it, trust me.

I'm not saying you have to be friends with everyone. I'm not saying you have to like everyone. But it's up to you to think about how you behave. Are you making someone else's day worse? Or better? Do you really think it's going to make you more popular to make someone else seem less cool?

I think a lot of you are mean because you are scared. You are scared you might seem weird or different from everyone else. You are scared no one is going to like you or someone is going to point out a strange habit of yours. I get it. I really do. And it's okay to feel a little bit scared. That's not the problem. The problem is what you do when you are scared.

For some kids, they simply aren't mature enough to cope with their own faults and become the bully so they won't get hurt themselves. That is the coward's way out. However, some kids are mature enough to do the opposite. They know people in general have flaws, and that everyone is working on themselves in some way. They have the compassion to offer a seat at their table to someone who needs it, or to partner up with other kids besides their close circle of friends. They're the kids who make sure everyone is having fun at recess, and always make conversation with whoever is around them. Sure, being a bully is the easy way out. But easy doesn't always mean right.

So, in a world of people who often take the easy routes in life, why not push yourself to take the right one?

Olivia

VIII
Pills

While I was trying to socially survive middle school, my mother had been researching physicians and found Dr. Richard Horowitz, who was renowned for his success in helping seriously ill Lyme patients. The only problem was that this doctor was thousands of miles away from where we lived—and the waiting list to see him was ten years long. Still, my mother got us on it—and I held on to the idea that maybe by the time I graduated college I would get to see him and start finally feeling better.

But out of the blue one day, when my mother was in the grocery store, she got a call from Dr. Horowitz's office. "Holiday, my name is Jane. I am Dr. Horowitz's assistant. We've been hearing about your daughter Olivia and these social media things she's doing in regards to the Lyme Challenge. She is amazing! You must be so proud of her. Dr. Horowitz is coming to Denver for a conference and would like to meet Olivia. Would that be possible?"

My mom nearly screamed in the middle of the grocery store but she managed to keep it together. "Yes, that would work just fine," she answered, trying to keep the obvious excitement out of her voice.

"Okay, I'll call you back and give you the information about where you can go get your tickets to hear him speak," Jane explained.

"Great," said my mother, barely able to speak. But just before she hung up the phone, she got an amazing idea. "How is Dr. Horowitz getting from the airport to the hotel?"

"Why do you want to know?"

"Oh, I'm so sorry if I overstepped my bounds, but I'm more than happy to pick him up and take him to the hotel."

There was silence on the other end of the line.

"I promise I won't kidnap him!" joked my mom. But still she was already planning on talking to the doctor in the car. Maybe it would be rush hour. Maybe she would have time to question him about treatments for Lyme disease.

"I'll ask the doc," Jane finally responded. "We'll get back to you."

"I'm just so grateful for all he is doing for Lyme disease patients that I want to help," explained my mother, which was true. What she didn't say was that she was also going to bring all of my medical records with her. The stack was over a foot high by now. But if there was any way she could get Dr. Horowitz to look at them, she'd make it happen.

Jane called back a little while later and said the doctor was happy to have her drive him from the airport to his hotel. My mom screamed when she got off the phone.

"Get the car washed!" my dad suggested when he heard the news.

My mom got bottled water and snacks for Dr. Horowitz. And she put them right next to the giant pile of my medical records. We made a sign together so Dr. Horowitz could find her when he got off the plane.

"I hear Olivia has Lyme disease," he said as soon as he was settled in the car. He glanced at the records. He immediately began asking my mom a whole bunch of questions. When was I diagnosed? What medicines had I been on? For how long?

"Has she had this test?" he asked my mom. "And this one?"

I hadn't had any of them. No doctor had ever thought to order them.

"Has she tried this antibiotic? Or this drug?"

Nope. Nope. And nope again.

Dr. Horowitz sighed and shook his head. They were almost at the hotel. He told her about how his wife had been sick with Lyme disease. His work is very personal to him.

My mom said a silent prayer to her godmother, who had passed the previous summer. "Please, please Kathy, let Dr. Horowitz help us."

"You know, Holiday," said Dr. Horowitz just that moment. "I don't have any plans tonight. Why don't we get dinner and keep on talking about Olivia? Maybe we can figure something out?"

Being a doctor isn't just a job for Dr. Horowitz. It's a mission. I think he dreams about treating people with Lyme disease and making sure his wife gets better. And maybe sometimes he has nightmares about it, too. But he's trying to treat everyone he can, however he can.

While Dr. Horowitz was checking in at the hotel, my mom called my dad and me. "We're having dinner!" she whispered. "He is telling me so much about Lyme! He is going to review your records while we eat!"

Of course, the documents were filled to the brim with therapist recommendations and dehydration diagnoses. Dr. Horowitz was unfazed, having seen those things before.

"Okay," he finally said, "this is incredible. I mean, fifty-one doctors? Wow. How about you visit me on a Sunday? That way, I will not kick anybody off the waiting list, since I don't work on Sundays. But tomorrow I want to meet Olivia. Why don't you both come to the summit? As my guests of course."

Little did I know that I would make my first speech about Lyme disease to an audience of over two hundred doctors. Right on the spot.

My parents and I were sitting there amongst all of these very serious doctors and scientists, with their laptops open and pens in hand. Dr. Horowitz was up on stage, having just given an incredible speech. He looked down at me, and simply said, "After I am done talking, I would like to introduce you all to my new friend, Olivia Goodreau. She will share with you her Lyme disease story. And she is a perfect example of how this disease can become part of anyone's life."

My eyes widened as I realized that I would have to give a decent speech in order to not embarrass Dr. Horowitz in front of the entire audience. I grabbed a napkin and began scribbling down some points. I was twelve, I didn't know how to do this. Public speaking was covered in eighth grade at our school. As I jotted down more notes, part of me was relieved that I could finally share my story where at least someone was bound to listen. I had dreamed of this moment, but not like this. Not where I only had ten minutes until the top doctors in the country would be focused on me.

It felt like only a few seconds until I could hear the audience applaud, signaling the end of the speech. I glanced up, and he invited me to join him on stage. I walked up onto the platform, worried that I would trip or pass out in front of everyone. I held onto the little napkin so tight that my knuckles were white. He bent the microphone down so that I could talk into it, the podium almost as tall as I was. With a smile, Dr. Horowitz took a step back, gesturing for me to begin.

"You can do this," he whispered to me with his New York accent.

It's funny, actually. How I started my speech then is a key part of my speeches now. I carried that intro with me, word for word, because they made such an impact on that audience. Only now, thanks to Dr. Horowitz, my talk isn't just about getting sick, it's also about getting better.

"Hi, my name is Olivia Goodreau and I was bitten by a tick at the Lake of the Ozarks when I was seven years old. I did not see the tick, and I did not get a bull's-eye rash. A few weeks later, I started to feel flu-like symptoms. I felt awful. I had CAT scans, MRIs, EKGs, liver biopsies, spinal taps, copper tests.

I saw over fifty doctors here in Colorado. Then, eighteen months later when I was in third grade, I was diagnosed with Lyme disease. But the diagnosis wasn't a happily ever after story. Because nobody knew how to treat me."

It was a turning point in my life.

For so long nobody had believed me and now I was talking to hundreds of doctors at once. It was one of the first times where I felt like the tide had turned. I wasn't trying to have my voice heard anymore. Now, people were leaning in, trying to hear me.

A month later we flew to New York to meet with Dr. Horowitz on a Sunday, when his office was closed.

"Bring snacks," he advised us.

"Why?"

"Visits take a long time and you may get hungry."

I was used to seeing doctors for ten or fifteen minutes while they ordered tests, shrugged their shoulders, and gave up.

That first visit took six hours.

I thought that taking blood pressure was a simple thing. You sit down, they pump air into the sleeve, and then it's over in a minute or two. Boy, was I wrong. Dr. Horowitz took my blood pressure in all of these different ways. He took it when I was lying down, then standing up, then sitting. Almost instantly, he diagnosed me with Postural Orthostatic Tachycardia Syndrome, also known as POTS. He explained that while my blood pressure looked fine sitting, it changed drastically when lying down or standing, which was the cause for me getting dizzy and passing out. Every single detail was like that. He looked at everything, asked about everything. It turned out that not only did I have chronic Lyme disease, but I was basically a walking petri dish filled with other co-infections, anemia (shocker), and a rare blood disorder.

There's this Marvel character called The Watcher. He watches all of these different realities play out. How different choices lead to different actions and different destinies. I wonder if he had been watching all of the versions of me. The ones with and without Lyme. The ones who got diagnosed early and the ones who still don't know. The ones who got better and are completely fine now.

Turns out I'm in the reality where they said, "Her blood pressure isn't a problem. There doesn't seem to be anything the matter with her. She was probably dehydrated."

Dr. Horowitz seemed to change that reality almost overnight. He never assumed anything and always asked me to fill out a huge questionnaire whenever I visited him. He explained it all to me. "Here are your symptoms that you've presented with like last time I talked to you. Are they better, worse, the same? Are they gone? What new symptoms have shown up?"

And then at the end of our visit together, he asked, "Do you have any questions for me?"

After our first visit he put me on a regimen that included taking eighty-six pills a day. And getting used to it wasn't easy. The first time I took them, I did the normal human thing and threw them all up. I got down to the last pill, swallowed it, gagged, and the next thing you know my sink looked like a crime scene. So I had to start over. I quickly found out that taking them all at once wasn't working, so I left about five minutes in between every round of pills. I would organize them by shape, color, and size. I'd take the group of brightly colored pills, then the group of oval pills, then the chalky circular ones. I'd save the giant glutathione pills for last, mentally hyping myself up to take them. I began to challenge myself to see how fast I could take them all before I had to leave for school. Half an hour soon became twenty minutes, and eventually I could take them in ten minutes before I had to leave. A spoonful of sugar, or a little bit of Nutella, really did help the medicine go down.

And, slowly but surely, I was starting to feel better once again.

Dr. Horowitz would run tests to make sure the drugs were working and if they weren't, he would change them. In the past doctors would blame me if something wasn't going to plan. Not Dr. Horowitz. He was creative. He would mix things up. He knew everybody's body was different. He said he was making me a drug cocktail, which would be catered to my health, my immune system. It wasn't like a one-size-fits-all situation.

Dr. Horowitz is a funny, peaceful, very sweet person. And he has a real plan for healing me. He even told me what to do and what doctor to go to if something ever happened to him. But most of all, his patients actually get better. He's now like a special uncle to me, someone I trust for advice and help of all kinds. He's not just a doctor, he's family now. And I think a lot of his patients feel that way about him.

I wish everyone had a Dr. Horowitz in their life.

IX
LivLyme

The better I felt, the more I realized how sick everyone else was. I began to hear more and more about kids and adults who weren't able to find doctors like Dr. Horowitz and had to suffer alone or with the nagging of skeptical nurses. I heard that the biggest reason why kids were so sick was because they couldn't afford the treatments prescribed, let alone a Lyme-literate doctor to help them. I realized that I had never thought about costs; my parents took care of all of that. I wouldn't know for a long time just how much they had sacrificed in order to get the uninsured doctor's appointments, medicine, and tests that I needed.

Then one day, while I was scrolling through my mom's Facebook, I came across a story of a mom and her son who had Lyme. They were living in their car, having to sell their apartment for medication. They lost their home for a few pills.

"This isn't fair!" I told my mom the moment I found her. "There must be something we can do, right?"

I wanted to mail them all the money I had right on the spot. But my mom was the one who explained that they weren't the only ones having to go through that kind of sacrifice. There were families like that all over the country. All over the world.

"So how are we going to help them all?" I asked.

My grandmother and my mom were always doing things to help out our community. They raised money for teens who were homeless, for early childhood education, for all kinds of causes. They made phone calls, they put on big parties, they asked for donations, and they made a difference.

My mind was whirring. "What if we throw a gala? Like the ones you help throw. What if we invited everyone we knew in Denver? And we invited Dr. Horowitz to talk about Lyme disease? Then we could raise money to help lots of families, right? That's how you and Bebe do it."

I looked up at her, noticing the tired eyes that stared back at me. It didn't stop her, though, and she smiled. "That is a wonderful idea."

"We'll start a foundation. We'll raise money from all over the country. I don't want any family having to live in their car like that again."

My mom took a deep breath. "We can try, honey."

"And we can raise money for the scientists so they can do more research and find a cure. We can do that, too! Because if they can find a cure, everyone can finally get better. Even me."

My mother shook her head. "Olivia, I think you can do anything you set your mind to. You are going to need a non-profit organization to do all of this, however. What do you want to call it?"

"It's LivLyme."

"LivLyme?"

"Because my nickname is Liv," I explained, "and I'm living with Lyme. Boom. LivLyme."

"Starting a foundation is not easy. There's a lot of work that goes into it. So I need you to really think about all of this. Is this really what you want to do? Do you want to make this kind of commitment? You told me how you want to do ordinary kid things and let me tell you, having a foundation at twelve is not an ordinary kid thing."

Maybe I've read too much mythology and watched too many superhero movies but if there's one thing I know from them, it is that once something has changed you, you can't ever go back to normal. It took me a while to realize that. And superheroes don't waste their days wishing to be normal again. They give back. They help people. They make sure no one else has to go through what they did.

There was so much to do. My mom handled the paperwork, but I had to design a logo, figure out what we wanted the website to look like, and invite people to our first gala. Dr. Horowitz was thrilled to speak, but he could only come out on April 8th, so we had our gala date before our foundation.

But the best part was inviting my friends—Skylar and Amelia, Lucas and Walker—to be my junior host committee. We had to plan decorations and seating charts, the music and the food. We all met one weekend with the caterer at a hotel and she brought us all kinds of dishes to try out. We had to choose the options for the appetizers and the main course and the dessert, having to taste everything first. All of it was delicious—and the caterer was very innovative. Because she knew that lots of scientists would be coming to the event, she designed these tomato mozzarella kebabs that were stuck on a laboratory pipette. When you squeezed the pipette, balsamic vinegar oozed over the cheese. And I remember the scientists loving it, and some of the more serious ones even broke out in laughter at the clever idea. For dessert there was a chocolate cake with a little lime candy on top.

Finding a lime green dress turned out to be harder than I thought it would be. Most of them were very gaudy, like something a great aunt would wear. I needed something that wouldn't make me look like a bedazzled muppet. My friends and I must have gone to every single store in Denver but I finally found a dress that would suit me. In later years the junior host committee decided to just find dresses we really liked and wear lime green sashes instead, which was a lot less of a hassle. And at our most recent gala I just stuck with lime green shoes.

When the big night finally came, all my friends came over and my mother's best friend volunteered to do our hair and make-up. After we were all ready, we drove over to where the event would take place. We got there an hour early to make sure everything was perfect for our guests. And finally, it was time to open the doors.

So many people came. Not just friends and family from Denver but scientists from all over the country and people who cared passionately about finding a cure for this disease. There was even a delegation from Korea filming the whole event live on their phones so their friends back at home could watch. We had set up a silent auction in the back room and people were bidding on everything. Dr. Horowitz went right to business, instantly connecting with other scientists and even talking to a few people with Lyme disease, giving them advice and tips on how to start feeling better.

I talked about the family that had inspired me to start the foundation and what a hardship this disease could be for so many people. I explained how everyone in this room was able to help, and how they could make a difference in the world.

Later on in the night, the band Judah & the Lion began to play their new album, and most of the audience made their way to the center of the room to dance and talk more. I talked to so many people that night, shaking hands, telling my story over and over again. Every now and then I'd get to laugh with my friends, but most of the time I was with scientists or doctors or senators who had decided to come. The event ended at midnight, every auction item claimed by someone, and we were finally allowed to go home and sleep.

In that first gala, we raised over $200,000 and had over fifty families apply for help. And every year after, those numbers have grown. Hundreds and hundreds of people have asked for help from all over the country. And many of them have more than one child who is sick with Lyme.

We didn't have any large advertisements, so the fact that these people were finding us without billboards or commercials was huge. It meant that we were starting to get more popular in the Lyme world, and that families were so desperate to find anyone who could help.

Reading over the applications is one of the hardest parts of my job. Every year I end up a sobbing mess after reading through every single story. They were devastating. Some kids have daily seizures, while others are paralyzed. One family in particular had eight children, all with Lyme, and the parents were so busy taking care of them that they could barely work.

I called the mother of one grant recipient in New Mexico. I learned that most grant recipients think I'm a spam call and hang up the first time, so I identified myself as quickly as possible. "Hi! I'm Olivia Goodreau from the LivLyme foundation, and your son has been chosen for a grant!" I said in one breath, hoping it wasn't too late.

I heard silence on the other end of the line, which then turned into loud sobs. The woman could barely talk. "I'm in the car. I have to pull over or I'm gonna crash," she said at last. "I can't believe this. I can't believe this. We are finally going to get some help. My son is so sick, and the insurance won't cover anything. Will you talk to him, Olivia? Will you tell him how you are getting better? Will you give him some hope? That would mean the world to him."

Over the years I have talked to so many kids and so many families. It never gets any easier.

Families have so many other problems thanks to this illness. There have been divorces and court cases and legal battles. They've lost their life savings and their homes. They worry if their children will ever get better and have normal lives again. They don't just want money. They want hope.

We tried to fund as many families as we could. If we couldn't fund one family one year, we tried the next. We covered tests, doctors, medications and just about everything but service animals. Sadly, emotional support hamsters would not make the cut. While I love animals and know that my dogs helped me get through a lot, we would rather have our grant go to medication and doctor's visits over pets.

Sometimes we would fund one sibling who was sick and the next year another. Sometimes we called up our big donors and asked for extra help because a family was in a really terrible situation.

Each year we raised more and more money. But each year there were more sick kids and more families reaching out. It wasn't enough to just take care of the kids. We had to start supporting the scientists, too. We had to find a cure for Lyme disease. And I wanted to be part of making that happen.

X
The Trojan Horse

The one thing Dr. Horowitz told me not to do was get swept up in the politics of Lyme disease, because there is a lot of fighting between different groups about the best way to prevent it, diagnose it, and treat it. I was determined to be neutral, like Switzerland, when anyone asked me my opinion about various issues.

Until I met Colonel Nicole Malachowski.

She was the first female pilot to fly as part of the United States Air Force Thunderbirds Squadron. She's the real-life Captain Marvel. She's a fighter pilot, a total badass, and super smart. I think she even had the same haircut as Captain Marvel at one point. She is a total powerhouse—and she had her whole career cut short by Lyme disease. One day she woke up and she was completely paralyzed from the neck down. Another day she went to go get food for her cat, only to realize that she didn't even own a cat. For nine months she could barely walk or even speak. So, as you can imagine, she wasn't going to be flying anymore. She was medically retired from the work that had been her whole life. The government spent millions of dollars on her education and training only for a little bug to make her "unfit for duty."

Just like me, it took her forever to get diagnosed and treated for her symptoms. And, just like me, she decided to make a difference too. She now travels the world to advocate for other medically retired military personnel, pushing for better tick-prevention methods for all people who serve the US Military. She's the ambassador and mentor of the Air Force Wounded Warrior Program.

I first met her in Washington D.C., when we both spoke at the U.S. Department of Health and Human Services meeting for their Tick-Borne Disease Working Group. After the meeting, she told me that she was going to discuss her concerns about kids with Lyme. But after she saw me speak right before her, she decided to focus mainly on her work with the military. She gave me a photo of her in a fighter jet flying over the Washington Monument, which is now framed in my room. From that day on she has been one of my dearest and most inspiring friends I've ever had. Nicole even ended up joining the board for LivLyme. She taught me how to properly salute and told me stories of when she was active, like how she got her callsign "FiFi". She once told me that we were both "recruited by ticks", and I now use that in my speeches. It doesn't have a negative connotation like being "bitten by a tick" does. Her version sounds like a mission, a quest where only the bravest can go. And I like to think that we are both pretty brave.

I didn't want to get into politics—but sometimes politics is the only way you can get things done.

Through LivLyme we were meeting so many families who could not get insurance to cover their medical care. We knew that ticks were everywhere, all across the country and there are all kinds of tick-borne illnesses. Hundreds of kids get diagnosed with Lyme disease every day—and a whole bunch more are like me, going year after year, getting sicker and sicker without getting diagnosed.

When I went to Washington, I thought of myself as the Trojan horse. Here I was, this teenage girl who seemed so quiet and polite and nice. I wasn't a lobbyist. I wasn't a doctor. I didn't have an agenda for any political party. What I wanted to know was how many representatives and senators knew someone who had been affected by Lyme disease. Was it their daughter, their nephew, their aunt? Maybe it was someone they worked with. But who was going to do something about it?

Senator Susan Collins, a Republican, got behind our work because her friend Senator Kay Hagan, a Democrat, had died of Powassan Virus, which is another tick-borne disease.

I was in Washington with Nicole at the time and we had just gotten back to our hotel, having previously talked with multiple congressmen. Exhausted from the long day, we decided to compare and contrast our Lyme symptoms. Turns out we could both see the spirochetes in our eyes. They were like little corkscrews swimming across our pupils. Pretty gross—and a sign that the Lyme disease was still in our bodies and brains. But it was strangely nice to have someone I could talk about this stuff with, someone who understood.

But that night my phone buzzed. I looked down at my old, cracked screen and it said it was from D.C. so I figured I should answer it.

"Hello, this is Senator Susan Collins's aide. Am I speaking to Olivia Good-reau?"

"Y-yes," I answered, stunned. How did she find my number? I tugged at my mom's arm and pointed at the phone, which I switched to "speaker."

"Are you willing to meet with Senator Collins in her office?" asked the aide.

"Of course," I replied.

"Great. We will see you in thirty minutes."

"No problem." I gulped. It was already late in the day, and we were just hanging out at the hotel lobby. I was in sweatpants and a t-shirt, my hair a mess. A part of me wanted to go like this right over to her office and show the senator what someone with chronic illness really looks like at the end of the day. But I thought better of it and quickly got dressed and ready and I'm glad I did because, boy, was Senator Collins put together. Her office was immaculate, neat as a pin. Compared to the offices of other politicians, it was really striking. Every shelf was dusted, every folder in a precise pile.

She was organized. "I want you to help me," she said after shaking my hand. "I want you to help me get the Kay Hagan Tick Act passed. We are going to allocate $150 million for research into tick-borne illnesses. How does that sound?"

I was speechless.

"Olivia, I want you to spread the word to other representatives and congressmen and senators, because you seem like the kind of girl who gets things done."

"Really?" I gushed. I thought of all the courageous things Nicole had done as a colonel in the Air Force. This was now my own mission. "All right!" I agreed.

So I started going door to door through Congress. I started with people that we knew were already interested in Lyme disease and then I went to their friends. I would basically say something like, 'I just met with your buddy Senator So-and-so, and he said I should talk to you,' and then they would let me in to talk to them.

By this point I knew my speech like the back of my hand, "Hi, I'm Olivia Goodreau. I'm the founder of the LivLyme Foundation and I want to talk to you about Lyme disease." I didn't go in demanding something; I told them my story. My superpower was that a lot of people underestimated me. They probably thought I was some dumb-blonde stereotype, and being only a teen, they didn't view me as anything special. They were definitely caught off guard when I would go into Lyme disease with facts and statistics, having a plan for how they can help already set up.

In December of my freshman year in 2019, Susan Collins called me again. The Kay Hagan Act, a bipartisan bill, had been passed. Finally, there would be more money to study tick-borne diseases and figure out how to treat them.

But it wasn't over yet. I had completed one mission. But there was still a lot more that I had to do.

Dear Politicians,

I don't care whether you are a Democrat or a Republican. And neither do the ticks. I don't care if you think you are from a state that doesn't have a problem with Lyme disease. Here is what I know. You are going to be somewhere you think is just fine, out golfing, on a nature trip, working in your backyard, traveling with your family, and you might get bitten by a tick. So, the first thing I am going to ask you all is to stay safe. There's nothing you can do to help us if you are sick. Get informed about protecting yourself from ticks and tick-borne diseases—because the moment you do you are going to realize what a problem they are across our entire country.

I never saw a tick bite me. I never got a bull's-eye rash. I was in the Midwest, not on the East Coast. It took me years to get a diagnosis and begin getting treated for what is now a chronic illness.

We've got a lot of work to do together. We need to find a way to prevent tick-borne diseases and we need much better testing to determine if people have been exposed to them. We need comprehensive treatments that don't leave people sicker than before. We need to do a lot of research and find out what really works. Because we are losing people to this illness and we don't want to lose you guys, too.

I think if Lyme disease was more visible, if it gave you blisters like smallpox or rashes like measles, it would get a lot more attention. If it put you into the hospital right away like Covid, everybody would take note. People would be like, "Oh that's terrifying, let's do something." But Lyme is a chameleon disease. It hides in your body and it makes people sick in all kinds of different ways. Why am I fainting? Why do my joints hurt? Why can't I think? Why do I have digestive issues and heart problems out of the blue? We are losing people to tick-borne illnesses and we don't even know it.

But look at the super-powered effort we mustered during Covid. Why can't we do something like that for tick-borne illnesses? If we did more for prevention, we would save money spent on treating everyone who gets sick. If we did better at diagnosis, the treatment would be easier than it is when the disease becomes chronic. If we had better treatments, maybe we would save on hospitalizations.

Ticks don't discriminate; you should not discriminate either. They don't care if you are from a red district or a blue district. And so, do what the ticks do: don't discriminate. It's not hard.

Imagine what we could do if we all worked together on this.

Olivia

XI

Superheroes

When everyone found out I had a new doctor, they instantly assumed that I was better already. That I had been cured. A smile on my face must have meant that I was fine, right? Obviously, that wasn't the case. While it was true that I was starting to feel better, that didn't happen overnight. My medications were working for the most part, going from good, to bad, to worse, then back to good again. That can be known as "herxing", coined from Dr. Herxheimer who discovered the event. Dr. Horowitz had explained this to me before, but I didn't realize how bad I could get until I was on vacation.

My family had decided to go to a beach for spring break that year, and it was awful. Not for them, they were having a blast, but I found myself spending most of my time sleeping in a hammock or wishing I could join my family at the beach. I not only felt awful physically, but I also felt like I was wasting my time. My parents had finally decided to go somewhere fun to celebrate how far we had come, and all I could do was sleep. I couldn't play with my brothers, Jack and Will, even though I promised them that I would. They'd check on me and bring me seashells, and I felt miserable that I was making them worried too. They were three years old when I got sick, so they never really knew me as not being ill. Maybe a few memories here or there, but to them I was always like this. Mom and Dad were always concerned about me, and I know that at first, they probably thought they were favoring me over them. But on that trip, where we were *supposed* to have fun, I think they realized that my parents were doing all of this for a reason.

With all of the free time I had unfortunately acquired, my mind started to wander. There must be something out there that can help Lyme patients get better in an easier, faster, less painful way. Turns out my mother was thinking the same thing as she kept an eye on me from under an umbrella. And soon after we got home, we started to see what scientists were already working on treatments, and how LivLyme could support them.

There's this one iconic scene in *Spider-Man 2*, where Spider-Man has to stop a runaway train. He realizes that one web won't stop the train, so he shoots out multiple webs all over the sides of buildings in order to stop it. Dealing with Lyme disease is a little bit like that. We can't just focus on one area. One doctor or scientist wasn't going to solve everything. In order to stop the disease in its tracks, we have to combine the strengths of multiple doctors, medications, studies, and ideas. We have to connect with the community, researchers, and politicians. Before we could solve anything, we had to become a strong, united force.

So, let me give you the rundown of some of the superheroes I've met so far.

When I first met Dr. Neil Spector at Duke University I immediately thought of Bruce Banner. He couldn't turn into a giant raging green monster, but he was just as smart as Dr. Banner. He had been studying breast cancer, having already developed two medications for it, when Lyme disease almost killed him. He went from an active marathon runner to eventually losing his own heart to Lyme in the blink of an eye. After he got a full heart transplant, Dr. Spector decided to devote himself to curing what nearly killed him.

He showed me all around his labs and explained that he was curious about how certain kinds of infrared light might destroy the spirochetes. "We need to think outside of the box. You should come and join me," he said. "Finish up high school early and come to Duke!"

In a few short days he became one of my best friends. He started telling me about all the cutting-edge scientists I had to meet. I felt like I was starting to compile my own team of superheroes.

Next, I went to Stanford where Dr. Rajadas and his team were testing over 3,000 already FDA-approved drugs to see which ones might affect Lyme disease. They were working smarter, not harder, basically skipping the whole FDA drug approval process. They reminded me of some kind of spy agency, being able to test medicines from all over the world in order to find out what could help.

I went to Boston to meet Dr. Kim Lewis at Northeastern. He was studying how to deal with antimicrobial tolerance, which limits medication effects. He was the most intimidating doctor by far, extremely professional and serious for the majority of his lab tour. We later went to lunch together, and I was shocked to hear him make a proposition to me. "I will trade you a bite of my carrot cake for a bite of your chocolate cake, do we have a deal?"

I smiled, relieved to know that he had a little bit of humor. "We have a deal."

I met Dr. Eva Sapi at the University of New Haven. She had made a huge discovery about biofilms, which were like a forcefield around the Lyme spirochetes that stopped the medications from getting through. For years, doctors couldn't figure out why drugs weren't working, and Dr. Sapi made the discovery that we need to get past these biofilms first. She showed me her labs filled with zebra fish for testing, and we even had a pizza party with her team.

Dr. Sapi had been a professor at Yale when she got Lyme disease and like so many of us, her own illness inspired her research. And, like most of us, nobody believed her at first. She went to her department at Yale and said, "This is a pretty big thing and I think I can make a difference. Can I have some money to do research on Lyme disease?" And Yale basically said no. And so she decided to go somewhere where she would be supported. She was like Professor

McGonagall, except less stern and much funnier. She was kind and humble, making sure to surround herself with people who wanted to help her.

All of these scientists have come from many different backgrounds, having their own origin stories that have brought them where they are now. Through our fundraising with Liv-Lyme, we were able to give grants to these scientists to help them with their research and continue their journeys to becoming real-life superheroes.

Dear Scientists and Researchers,

I just want to say thank you for all that you do. Thank you for figuring out years ago that the reason so many kids in Connecticut had arthritis was because of a tick-borne illness. Thank you for investigating the Lyme spirochetes and figuring out how they make people sick. Thank you for inventing so many different kinds of medicines to treat so many different problems—many of which people with Lyme disease end up having.

Thank you for your patience and your persistence. Thank you for taking late night shifts and working on the weekends. If it weren't for you, I would never have had a test for Lyme disease, I would never have been able to take any of the eighty-six different medicines that made it possible for me to begin healing. I would have never gotten better.

All I want to ask of you is that you don't give up. Don't give up until we have better tests to diagnose Lyme, a vaccine that works against tick-borne illnesses, and treatments that are accessible and affordable for everyone. You guys have done so much already, and we know that you still have a long way to go.

So thank you for what you have done. And thank you for what you are trying to accomplish. We all count on you.

Olivia

XII
There's An App for That

We were back at the Lake of the Ozarks. I was finally able to enjoy the sun and boating in a way that I hadn't been able to since I had first gotten sick. We spent the entire day swimming, water skiing, and tubing until sunset. With sunburned faces and messy lake hair, my family and I finally docked the boat and headed inside to watch a movie. As the opening credits came up on the screen, my dog Mo wanted to go outside.

I got up and let him out to relieve himself and waited by the door. I watched the starry night as cicadas whirred in the distance. A few minutes later, Mo trotted back inside and flopped down in front of the couch. My brother started the movie back up, but quickly paused it again as he realized how weird Mo was acting. He was biting himself, rolling around on the floor and on the sides of the couch. The biting got worse, and he started to bleed.

I turned on the lights to see better and noticed hundreds of freckles all over his legs. Except they weren't freckles. Looking closer, I could see tiny little legs on each little black dot. They were ticks. In an instant, the entire family went into panic mode. I raced to grab tweezers while my mom grabbed a plastic bag. I started to pluck off the ticks, dropping them into the bag. Once I was positive I had checked every inch of Mo, I started to count the ticks. Ten. Twenty. Fifty. I ended up counting over two hundred ticks. In just a few minutes my dog got covered in two hundred ticks.

"Mom!" I shouted. "What kind of ticks are these? Where can we see what ticks are in the Ozarks?"

"Olivia, we have ticks in our house right now," my mom nearly yelled. "I'll answer your question tomorrow, but right now we need to get them off the damn dog and out of our damn house." She was already grabbing her keys and headed to the car, wanting to get Mo some Flea & Tick shampoo before the store closed. She came back at midnight, and we eventually finished combing every inch of the house and our bodies for ticks at around one in the morning.

Sleep didn't come easy, probably because I was hyperventilating about getting bitten again. I think I had a panic attack at some point in the night. But when the sun finally rose into the sky the next morning, I was already searching for answers.

I typed into the search bar: *What kinds of ticks are in Lake of the Ozarks, MO?*

Nothing came up.

"Mom!" I shouted from the computer. "There is no place you can go to figure out stuff about the ticks in your area, that's up to date anyway. A few places have these outdated general maps of the state but that's about it."

My mother was bleary-eyed and exhausted. "I guess no one has invented anything like that yet."

"I could do that."

"What?" said my mom, taking a sip of iced tea.

"I've gotta make one. An app. That tells you about the ticks in your area in real time. That helps you identify them and lets you know if they carry disease or not. And we could let all our scientists know what we find out, too, so they would have more information for their work, right?"

"You're gonna make an app?" asked my brother Will.

"Make it cool!" Jack grinned.

"It'll be the coolest tick app out there. Probably the only one too." Eight months later and the app, TickTracker, was ready to launch. My great-uncle connected me with some app designers he knew, and I told them about all of the features I wanted on it. It had to be super simple and easy for everyone to use. The more people that were able to use it, the more reliable the data would become. This meant making it in different languages.

And they did. We had deer hunters checking our app to see which parts of the forest were most infested with ticks. We had people reporting on the ticks in their backyards and local hiking trails. We even had a goat farmer in Pakistan who loved the app because now he could take better care of his herds.

The amount of tick data we had grew by the day. The CDC, along with numerous universities and companies started to share their data with us. We even got the Smithsonian Institute to give us their collection of data including over 200,000 ticks. As time went on, we finally had a reliable, real-time tick map.

I was encouraged to enter my app into The Opportunity Project, a four-teen-week tech sprint created by the U.S. Department of Health and Human Services in order to see what technologies were out there and solving world issues. There were scientists from MIT, Microsoft, Oracle, and IBM. And then there was me. We all set up booths and presented our problem-solving tech-nologies to judges in the White House. I remember having imposter syndrome the entire time I was there. I was the only one there that hadn't gone to college yet, or who hadn't gotten their Ph.D. at a renowned university. I was literally supposed to go on my middle school D.C. trip in a few weeks. And I could tell that the other contestants were thinking the same thing about me. They'd ask how old I was, or if I knew where I was going to college yet. They'd ask if I knew anyone in order to get a spot in the competition, if I had pulled a few strings so they could let a kid in.

I think we were all surprised when they announced that TickTracker had won.

To think I won against those big names was crazy. I almost didn't believe it. They all had absolutely incredible inventions, and to this day I still wonder how their research and inventions are doing out in the world.

The one thing we all had in common was our desire to help people. Many of those contestants had a personal reason that led them to creating their invention. They didn't have to spend fourteen weeks working tirelessly on their projects, but they did. Being in that historical blue room was like walking through both ancient history and the making of it. Every now and then I see some billboard or article about one of their inventions, and I can look at it knowing that I was there with them. That we were working for the same cause: helping humanity.

I would not have had the idea to create TickTracker if it hadn't been for Mo. We got him at the Ozarks, and his name stood for Missouri. He would wake me up every morning for school by laying on my pillow, giving me a 'Mohawk'. On the morning of the second LivLyme gala, my family and I were helping load supplies into our car when we witnessed Mo run out of the house to greet a dog across the street. None of us were prepared for him to get hit by a car. My dad rushed him to the vet while the rest of us tried to regain our composures and prepare for the gala that evening. I had to smile through that entire night, presenting my speech and giving awards as if Mo was completely fine. At midnight he passed away, his injuries being far too great for the vets to fix. It's crazy to think that a little black and white dog would spark an idea that would lead to a global app that has been helping people from all around the world. And I hope that somehow, Mo can look down and see all the good that has been done from it. He may have been a tiny dog with an underbite, but no hero is too small.

XIII
Center Stage

In the midst of managing my own treatment and my advocacy work were the ordinary challenges of growing up. I lost friends because of my illness and endured years of bullying and teasing. Doctors and teachers refused to believe I was really sick, and I struggled to explain to others what was happening to me.

One of the hardest things of all was that I was denied my top choice of high school because of both my illness and my advocacy.

I had all As. I had great test scores. I even had recommendations from scientists at Stanford and Duke University. I was starting to become a public figure, going on television talking about my app and tick-borne diseases. In my mind, I was thinking that with all of these things, I would have a great chance of getting in. Schools want app creators and advocates, right?

Wrong.

Ironically, it basically put a giant bull's eye right on me.

It was a beautiful day when admissions were announced. I was sitting on the couch with my entire family next to me. Even my dad left work early to be there for me. I felt pretty relaxed about everything. I couldn't imagine that I'd have a problem. It felt like an eternity, but after refreshing the page on my laptop, the results were posted.

I looked down at the screen.

I'd been waitlisted.

The girl who I had tutored in math for two years had got accepted. The boy who openly cheated on every test and received multiple suspensions got accepted. The girl who told everyone she would be moving in a year got accepted. Skylar got accepted.

I got this news as everyone on the group chat shared their results, excited to all be together. They kept on asking if I got in, and I was too embarrassed to reply.

It felt like I'd been punched in the gut. I'd put up with so much, having to work twice as hard just to get good grades while simultaneously going through treatments. And the one thing that had kept me going was getting into the high school of my choice so I could be with my friends. One tear landed on the keyboard, then another. And soon I couldn't stop. All of my friends knew where they were going and I was left alone, again.

My mom immediately started making calls to figure out what was going on. The guidance counselor at my middle school couldn't make any sense of it. She'd never seen something like this happen. "We don't know what's going on either. We can't believe she didn't get in; we don't know what's happening."

When I finally told my friends, they couldn't believe it either. "I thought you would've gotten in before me. What happened?"

Dr. Horowitz, who had written a recommendation for me, was furious. He was ready to fly out to Denver and give the Admissions Committee a stern talking to. Dr. Spector told me to just get my GED and come to Duke University to work with him. Honestly, it sounded like the best option at that point. Dr. Spector wrote an email to the Head of Admissions and the Head of School and said, "Wow, you must have the most amazing applicants that you did not have space for this young woman."

School felt intolerable. All my friends knew where they were going, and I wasn't going anywhere. It was too late in the spring to even apply anywhere else. And even if I did get in from the waitlist, did I really want to go somewhere that didn't want me?

The guidance counselor at school told me to look at an all-girls school called St. Mary's. "It has fabulous academics," she told me. "And real girl power."

But I wanted to have an actual high school experience. I wanted a coed school. Having guy friends was a blessing to me throughout middle school. They weren't part of any mean girl regime, and they didn't even care about Lyme disease. And how was I supposed to date anyone if I was stuck at an all-girls religious school?

Eventually, I agreed to go and at least talk to St. Mary's. After all, it had been a woman doctor who had finally diagnosed me after fifty clueless men. I thought about Dr. Eva Sapi leaving her position at Yale to pursue the research that mattered to her. I thought about Nicole and her fighter jet. Maybe I would meet people like them at this school.

The Admissions Officer at St. Mary's wanted to know why I didn't want to go to any of the more selective high schools and when we told them that I had been waitlisted at my top choice, she was horrified. She couldn't believe it. "Do not even worry about filling out an application," she told my mom. "Just send over her transcripts and we'll talk to Olivia tomorrow."

The next day, I had an interview with the local news to talk about Lyme Disease Awareness Month. As I was talking with the interviewer live on television, I looked behind the stage and saw my mom crying behind the camera. When the segment was finally finished, I rushed to her side, thinking that someone had died in the family. She gave me her phone and I saw the email that I had been accepted into St. Mary's. In less than a day. I nearly cried too, but I had to take pictures with the news anchor, so those tears would have to wait for the car. The principal had seen me on the news in that very exact moment and she was eager to help me with my foundation and my advocacy.

I made the executive decision that I was going to keep my illness a secret at this new school. This was my chance to start over completely, with new people and a new setting. I would finally be normal. Maybe I could just be a teenager. Play volleyball. Do my homework. Go to parties. Maybe even, somehow, go on a date. So, I went to St. Mary's saying I was not going to talk about anything Lyme-related unless someone directly asked me. Or maybe I would lie about that, too.

In all honesty, I have never been a very religious person. I didn't have the strength to go to church on Sundays because I was so sick. My first-ever mass was with my entire school on our retreat. The conversation topic was our thoughts on what it meant to be a community of faith. An older student got up and talked about how this question didn't have anything to do with what you necessarily believed but rather how you behaved. What did it mean to live with sincerity, excellence, and joy? What did it mean to work for justice, freedom, and truth? I was unexpectedly inspired. The new kids were not talking just about where they went over the summer but what they wanted to do with their lives. They were sharing their experiences with such honesty that I felt genuinely moved. I'd never been to a school like this.

When I told my third-grade classmates about Lyme disease, it was a disaster. That event was what caused me years of being teased. But since then I had gotten a lot better about public speaking, and all of the girls here seemed to be speaking with such integrity and trust. Maybe it was time I try that again.

I'd already made some friends on the volleyball team, along with seniors that the school assigned to us to be our 'big sisters'. Maybe that was the push that got me onto my feet and walking up to the podium. Maybe that was what gave me the courage to start talking. I told my classmates about my illness and how it had inspired me to help others, that maybe that's what its purpose was. I told them about my foundation and giving money to struggling families to pay for their medical care. I talked about passing bills and going around the country to spread awareness. I even shared my goal of finding a cure.

It all just came pouring out of me. In the beginning, my legs were shaking, and I was stuttering, memories of the last time I did this flooding my head. But as I continued to talk, I felt grounded, unmoving.

And I talked about what the community meant to me. Not the community of classmates I'd known but the community of people all working together towards a goal—the doctors, the scientists, the politicians, and the Lyme patients and activists. My community stretched all around the country, all around the world. Without my community, I would have been totally lost.

"It's people like you who have been supporting me throughout my journey. And I'm forever grateful to those people. And so I want to give back to everyone who needs a friend." I finished.

What would everyone think?

For a moment there was silence. I thought that I completely messed up. That I would have to endure another four years of rumors. But then, the quiet sound of clapping rang from the back of the room. I looked to find an older teacher seated in the last row, their big round glasses reflecting the ceiling lights. In a matter of moments, the whole school began to applaud. Some of my volleyball friends were crying, which made me tear up. Teachers came up and hugged me later. I was invited to join a club or two. Another girl told me about her cousin with Lyme. And one girl stared at me, her eyes wide and said, "I was sure I'd be the only girl with Lyme disease here. I can't believe you are in my class!"

All day long girls were coming up to me and asking about ticks and Lyme disease and going to Washington. It wasn't in a mocking tone, it was genuine curiosity. I felt supported. They didn't ask why I looked fine. Maybe this school was right for me after all. Maybe I was finally at a place where I would be supported, encouraged, and inspired. No one seemed worried. No one seemed to think I was lying. No one seemed to flinch at being around me. No one called me contagious. The entire time I was thinking to myself: Finally.

XIV
Butterflies

When Covid-19 struck the world, it changed my life along with everyone else's. I wasn't traveling around the country anymore or giving speeches. I was already limited in having a high school experience because I was at an all-girls school, and now I couldn't even go to class. But the one thing that Covid took away from me was one of my heroes. One of my best friends.

Dr. Spector, who had been such a mentor to me, who I had dreamed of working on a cure with at Duke, passed away due to the outbreak. He had already lost his heart due to Lyme disease, and then on top of that, he got Covid. With an already weakened immune system, his Lyme flared up as well. He didn't make it.

I still text him, even though I know he will never respond. I just sent him a text that I toured Duke, actually. His amazing wife had once told me that whenever she sees a butterfly, she thinks of him. And for all that butterflies represent throughout history, I can see why.

***

Despite going to an all-girls high school in the middle of a pandemic, I was having a pretty normal teenage life. The Covid vaccine was created and we were back to parties and dating and football games and even unexpected kisses.

One day, someone added me on Snapchat, which was now the way to meet new people while in quarantine.

I looked at his name: Peter.

I shrugged. I had heard of him before, and I didn't really care at that point, so why not?

He had black messy hair and grey-blue eyes. He was good-looking, I'll admit, but for some reason, I was convinced he was short. I mean, really short. How was I supposed to know? I only saw pictures of him and there was no way I was going to ask him his height out of the blue. Still, he talked to me nearly every day, asking me tons of questions about my life.

A few weeks went by with us talking with one another and trying to figure out if we would ever meet each other in person. My friend was having a backyard party, one of the rare events where my friends and I got to meet guys from other schools.

I didn't expect Peter to be there.

"Oh, have you met Peter?" My friend, Maribel, asked, "He goes to the same school as my boyfriend; they're actually in a lot of classes together."

The first thing I noticed was that Peter was definitely not a short person. He towered over most of the kids there.

"It is nice to finally meet in person, Olivia." He said with a smile.

"Agreed." I laughed.

After that night, Peter seemed to keep appearing on our group's adventures. I eventually made the bold move and asked him to come to my school's prom, held at the aquarium. He said yes, and I invited him over to my house so we could talk more about the event.

When Peter first came over to my home, I figured I would give him a tour around the house. His eyes wandered to the photos and awards in the family office.

"There are so many magazine articles about you," he said. "I didn't realize how famous you are. I had no idea that there was an Olivia Goodreau Day in Colorado. What did you do to get so famous?"

My heart dropped. I didn't want to go there, especially on the night of prom. But it was too late now. I briefly told him my story. I was internally glad to get it over with, so if this thing continued there would be no big secrets. He didn't seem too fazed by it, which was shocking. He just kept on asking more questions, pointing out all of the awards and pictures of celebrities on the shelves. And then it was over, we moved on to the next room in the house.

Prom was amazing. We met up with the rest of my friend group and took pictures before going to the party. We danced until our feet hurt and then went to play laser tag afterwards. We were a deadly duo, easily gaining the most points in every round.

At some point in the night, I turned towards him. "You look like young Logan Lerman," I admitted. I mean, he really did.

"Not so much," he laughed. "Okay, maybe I'm the Dollar Store version of Logan Lerman. I'll give you that."

Peter and I ended up dating. We saw each other nearly every day over the summer, going on vacations with both his family and mine, and hanging out with our friend groups. We went to the amusement parks and museum, and even to an animal shelter to pet dogs for a day. It was convenient that we had such a large friend group made up of kids from different schools. Everyone already knew and liked each other, so there were no awkward introductions to be had. We went on a road trip to the beach with some of our friends, staying at the house of one of their relatives and spending time in the ocean whenever we could. We brought a polaroid camera everywhere we went, each taking pictures that would cover our walls.

During all of the fun adventures I experience with Peter, I still had to take pills. I thought that it would gross him out and that I would be better off taking them in private. One night, however, he proved me wrong.

We were over at my house, binge-watching the new season of *Yellowstone*. Both of us had fallen asleep on the living room couch when the sound of a phone alarm startled us awake. Peter looked at the time. It was midnight, and he was supposed to be home at midnight.

As he was getting on his shoes, I went over to the kitchen counter and grabbed my large case of pills. I figured that once I walked Peter to the front door, I could take them upstairs.

"Do you still have to take those?" I heard him ask as he turned off the TV.

"Yep." I sighed, prepared to walk him to the door. However, the pill box that I held in my hand was different from the regular one. It was lighter.

Dr. Horowitz had decided to have me partake in something called a Dapsone Protocol. Dapsone was a one-hundred-year-old leprosy drug, and he had discovered that it worked miracles on people like me. Instead of taking eighty-six pills a day, every day, the treatment consisted of only forty-two various probiotics, antibiotics, and supplements. The antibiotics fought the biofilms or little shields around the bacteria. The probiotics helped my gut survive the grueling process, and the supplements were to ensure that I wasn't harming myself in the process of fighting the diseases inside me. Dr. Horowitz had come to the conclusion that you needed all three to truly make a stand against tick-borne diseases. I had come to a point in my treatment where I was to take four times the normal dosage of Dapsone, making this week the most difficult one yet.

"Where do you normally take them?" He asked, walking over to me.

"Just my room, why?" I asked. I tried not to look at the box as I recalled the sickly plastic-like taste that would soon consume my senses.

"Let's go then." He said and whisked the pill case away from me, grabbing a blue Gatorade before heading upstairs. My heart started to race, and a familiar sense of dread washed over me.

"Peter, you have to go. Your parents will be pissed!" I whisper-yelled, following close behind.

"This is more important." We got to my room, and he sat down on the edge of my bed, opening the little section of the case that read 'Sunday: Night.' He then opened the Gatorade. "You said that you organize your pills. Show me how you do it."

I grabbed four brightly-colored pills, "Well…okay, if they're colorful like this, then they go together. If they're the same kind, like those four Glutathione, then they go together. Oh, and also if they're round." I don't know why, but as I was explaining my organization methods to him, I started to get emotional. Pill-taking was a very private thing for me. I normally didn't take them in front of anyone, not even my parents. And none of my friends had ever been as invested as Peter was right now. I could feel stinging tears form at the corners of my eyes as I took a handful of pills. How embarrassing.

Yet, when I tried to see if Peter would laugh at me or give me a look of disgust, I was met with another set of tear-filled eyes. He was crying? Why?

"Are you okay?" I sniffled.

He gave me a small kiss, and I tasted the saltiness of tears that weren't my own. "Yeah, I'm okay."

Our night continued with him intently watching me organize and take pills as he held onto the pill case and Gatorade bottle. He even held a handful of pills, which I regretfully told him were the gross, oozing kind. He didn't seem to care even when they had stained his palm orange and blue.

When I was finally finished, I quickly walked him down to the door. As I watched him get inside his car, I sank to the floor, sobbing. Ever since I had gotten sick, no one had ever done that for me. I quickly did the math in my head, realizing that I had taken over 200,000 pills over the course of a decade alone. And then Peter showed up, being the first person to witness it. He was the first person, besides my family, who actually showed me that they cared. Middle school was filled with 'get well soon' wishes at best, and high school wasn't any better. I didn't have friends who would wait patiently for me to take my medicine without giving off hints that they were annoyed or grossed out. Peter, however, was different.

I felt so lucky. So lucky that I not only had such a caring family but also such a caring and understanding boyfriend. I felt so lucky that I could count on so many people.

And after that night, I somehow started to feel more normal than ever. I felt so loved, so supported, that I felt like I almost didn't have Lyme disease. When the Dapsone Protocol finally ended, I truly felt better. I had a follow-up appointment with Dr. Horowitz to tell him the good news, and he responded with a word I never thought I would hear. Remission.

But wait. I wasn't finished. My story isn't over yet.

I couldn't simply turn a blind eye to the problem, even if I wanted to. That would be betraying not only my health and everything that I have worked for, but also the people that I made promises to. I know that tick-borne diseases will remain in the back of my mind even when I am feeling amazing. I know that I will keep thinking about all of the sick, undiagnosed, and untreated people with tick-borne illnesses. I cannot rest until everyone else is able to. I must finish what I started.

That one night with Peter, when I finally watched him leave, something caught my attention as I walked into my room for the second time. A soft, flittering noise was coming from the window. I walked over to close it, thinking that a branch was scraping against the screen, but when my hands reached the window sill I paused.

There was a little white butterfly on the screen.

I smiled, deciding to sleep with the window left open.

Dear Significant Other,

First of all, thank you. Thank you for being by our side and trying your best to understand what we are going through. It truly means a lot to us when we see you be open about our illnesses or conditions rather than close-minded or skeptical. Being with you makes us feel normal. Even if it's on FaceTime, your presence really does matter to us. It allows us to loosen up and almost forget that we are sick. So, if we don't talk about our illness often, it is not because we are trying to hide secrets from you. We simply just want to bask in that feeling of being alright. We want to do normal things, like laugh with you and make memories. We don't want to constantly talk about hospital trips and medications. So no, we aren't keeping secrets. Of course, we will discuss some things and always keep you updated on important stuff, but for the most part, we just want to feel normal with you.

Still, sometimes we are going to have sick days, and it's not your fault. Don't assume you've done something wrong or we don't like you anymore if we are acting off. Some days are bad, and even though we might put on a smile for you, internally, we are in pain. We don't necessarily want to tell you that we spent the whole morning throwing up or that we feel like we are going to pass out, or that the doctor just told us the medicine isn't working anymore. We don't want you to worry.

When we do explain what we are dealing with at that moment, it's because we feel close and safe with you. But we do not expect you to fix everything and solve medical problems that even our doctors don't know how to deal with. And please, don't tell us we should just take an Advil or drink more water or whatever. Most of the time we just want you to listen. We don't want to make you feel like you have to fix us right then and there, but listening to us is one of the best things you can do.

Just having you by our sides, supporting us and loving us, is already making us feel better. Even if it's by a tiny bit, your presence matters.

For most of us, the little things you do make the biggest difference.

And we are so thankful for you.

Olivia

XV
The Sunset

I hope within ten years I will be able to invite you, the reader, to a beach party. It's going to be at sunset on the West Coast and we'll sit at the edge of the beach, the waves lapping at our feet, and watch the sun drop into the ocean.

I'm going to invite my family and friends who stuck by me, the teachers and doctors who helped me and all the scientists who made this special day possible. Dr. Horowitz will be there laughing and telling stories. He'll be so relaxed, playing his guitar with his wife instead of being chronically overworked with sick Lyme patients. Lucas and Walker will be cooking up some kind of trouble together like they normally do, maybe trying to catch seagulls. Jack and Will will definitely help them. My family will be making sure everyone gets enough to eat. Colonel Nicole Malachowski, healed at last, will fly over us in a fighter jet. What are we celebrating? A complete cure for Lyme disease.

I mean, an efficient, affordable, easy cure for everyone. It doesn't matter to me if it is a drug or a vaccine, as long as it is able to cure anybody that needs it, make the term 'Lyme disease' seem as trivial as a head cold and eradicate the fear of suffering from a tick-borne illness. Forever.

I don't need to go fight for health care and research in Washington anymore. I don't have to meet with scientists to talk about possible treatments. I don't have to visit a doctor every month and detail my new symptoms and my old symptoms. Because I'm cured. Completely better. And so is everyone. And I don't even have to think about Lyme disease ever again. And you don't either.

If you get it, you can go to the pharmacy and say, "Hey, I got bitten by a tick. Can I have the nasal spray? And then I'm good." Or you pick up the pill and take it for three days. Something like that. It'll be cheap, easy, no big deal.

And out there on the beach as the ocean reflects hues of pink and orange, I'll be filled with relief. The kind you feel when you finish a lengthy paper or ace a big test you spent hours studying for. The only difference is that I had made this assignment a part of my life for years. But it will finally be done, and I'll finally get to feel free.

The sunset will be beautiful, turning the ocean itself into a sea of glistening gold. I know I'll see a butterfly, with wings of navy and light blue. And the moment I see it I'll know that it's a sign from Dr. Spector telling me that I can finally rest. I'll turn to everyone who has come that night and say, "All right, guys, it was a good run, a good journey. Memories were made. But I hope to never talk to you all about Lyme disease ever again."

I can see the doctors and scientists congratulating each other and raising a toast to their teamwork. Everyone is talking away and celebrating. And as the last rays of the sun disappear, that's what I'll do. Disappear.

I'm going to leave my own party early, as crazy as it sounds, and I'm going to go sit on the beach to watch the sky turn to a deep purple as little twinkling pinpricks of stars starting to become visible.

What will I do with the rest of my life? Maybe I will go into public health and continue to help others suffering from different diseases. Maybe I'll become a senator, advocating for and helping different communities across the country. Or maybe I'll go international, and work for the World Health Organization. And if I have time to do something else, I just might become a diving instructor, guiding people beneath the sea, showing them the hidden worlds that I fell in love with. Maybe I'll do all of that.

That will be tomorrow's adventure.

Acknowledgments

I would not be where I am today if it were not for the people in my life who supported me along the way. Firstly, I would like to thank my family for sticking by my side.

My mother, Holiday, has been my caretaker, appointment maker, and pill organizer for over a decade, and one day I hope to relieve her of that responsibility. She has been there on my best and worst days, watching me speak at the White House and comforting me whenever I end up in the hospital. When everyone else gave up on trying to diagnose me, she pushed for more tests and ideas. She saved my life, and I couldn't thank her more for that.

My Dad, Stan, is the rock of our family. He cared for my brothers when I was in the hospital with my mom. He works tirelessly to make sure I can afford the medications to feel better. But most importantly, he is always there to listen to me. Whether I need life advice or simply want to know how to change a tire, my dad has always offered a helping hand wherever he can. On top of that, he always tries his best to make my brothers and me smile, and I couldn't be more honored to call him my father.

My younger twin brothers, Jack and Will, do not remember me not being sick. They have been my biggest supporters, showing me so much love and appreciation. I am so lucky to be their big sister, and I am so proud of who they are becoming.

My grandmother, Bebe, is an astonishing woman. She had many adversaries throughout her life and decided to utilize them to do good in the world. She is also very involved in the world of non-profits, and I would not have had the courage to start one of my own if I had not witnessed her and my mother be so invested in giving to the community.

I would like to thank my friends for never leaving my side. When others bought into rumors or simply drifted away for other reasons, I am so lucky they chose to stick with me and help me. Going to school would not have been possible without them, and I am truly honored to have such a fantastic group of friends to depend on.

My current health would not have been achieved if it were not for the brilliant mind of Dr. Horowitz. He never ceases to develop new treatment plans as he works on finding the closest thing to a cure. I owe my life and my health to him.

If it were not for Ms. Cheadle's concern for my health, it might have taken even longer to be diagnosed with Lyme. She and teachers like Mr. Cauldwell, Ms. James, and Ms. Naughton were why I pushed past the world of 'mean girls' and found a different way to thrive academically. They went above and beyond the standard requirements of teachers to help me, and I could not be more grateful to have been in their classes.

I would also like to thank Nurse Megan for always making her office a safe place for me to go to. Having the ability to take breaks and rest throughout the school day helped me not only physically but also mentally.

Over many years of activism within the tick-borne disease community, I have met many exceptionally talented people. They have each shaped who I am today and have given me the wisdom of their experiences to hold and pass on to others.

For years, Colonel Malachowski has been sharing with me the awe-inspiring knowledge that she has gained from her struggles. Not only is she someone I know I can go to when I need advice, but she always makes me smile with her tales of being in the Air Force. I am honored to be "recruited by a tick" with her, and I know our friendship is unbreakable.

I would like to thank all the scientists I have met. The kindness and openness they showed me when I got to tour their labs solidified my hope in finding new cures and inspired me to pursue research in college. Scientists like Dr. Sapi, Dr. Rajadas, Dr. Haystead, Dr. Embers, Dr. Lewis, and countless others are incredibly unwavering in their efforts to find better treatments, and I am honored to call them my friends.

Dr. Spector was also one of those incredible scientists. However, he was also my mentor and dearest friend. Out of all of the people that I had met who suffered from Lyme disease, it is undeniable that he suffered the most. Yet, he undoubtedly showed the most compassion and devotion to understanding the thing that took his heart. Dr. Spector had every right to be bitter about his situation, yet he never was. We can all agree that he left this world too soon. However, his time on this planet was well-spent. I am so lucky to have known Dr. Spector and have created an extraordinary friendship with him.

TickTracker, LonghaulTracker, TickTickBoom, TickTracker-Pro, and TickMojis would not possible if it were not for my app developer, Jeff, and his incredible team. Thank you for developing these incredible technologies and traveling around the country with me to spread awareness everywhere we go.

I'd like to thank Dr. Honey for the unwavering support and encouragement she has shown me throughout the years. Additionally, I would like to thank Dr. Visser for the compassion and honesty she has demonstrated to the tick-borne disease community and myself. These incredible women inspire me daily, and I hope to be like them as I grow up.

I'd like to give a special thanks to Alexandra Cohen. She was one of the first people to believe in me and my apps, and I could not be more grateful to have her as a friend.

I would like to thank Anne Marie O'Farrell for believing in my story and showing me the world of literacy and book writing. I would also like to thank Perdita Finn for helping me put my story on paper through hours of long, therapeutic calls.

Lastly, I would like to thank everyone who has supported me and my non-profit. Whether you are new to the Lyme disease community or have been here longer than I have, I appreciate your compassion and determination to find a cure for tick-borne diseases. Every one of you is an inspiration to me.

Glossary of Terms

ADHD — Attention Deficit Hyperactivity Disorder (ADHD) is one of the most common neurodevelopmental disorders of childhood. It is usually first diagnosed in childhood and often lasts into adulthood. Children with ADHD may have trouble paying attention, controlling impulsive behaviors (may act without thinking about what the result will be), or be overly active.

Air Force Wounded Warrior Program — Air Force Wounded Warrior (AFW2) Program works together with the Air Force Survivor Assistance Program, Airman & Family Readiness Centers and the Air Force Medical Service to provide concentrated non-medical care and support for seriously or very seriously wounded, ill and injured Airmen, Guardians, Caregivers and their families as they recover and transition back to duty or into civilian life.

ALS — Amyotrophic Lateral Sclerosis (ALS), also known as motor neuron disease (MND) or Lou Gehrig's disease, is a neurodegenerative disease that results in the progressive loss of motor neurons that control voluntary muscles. ALS is the most common form of the motor neuron diseases.

ALS-Ice Bucket Challenge — The Ice Bucket Challenge, sometimes called the ALS Ice Bucket Challenge, is an activity involving the pouring of a bucket of ice water over a person's head, either by another person or self-administered, to promote awareness of the disease amyotrophic lateral sclerosis (ALS, also known as motor neuron disease or Lou Gehrig's disease) and encourage donations to research. Learn more at www.als.org.

Antibiotics — An antibiotic is a type of antimicrobial substance active against bacteria.

Arthritis — Arthritis is a term often used to mean any disorder that affects joints.

Babesia — is a tiny parasite that infects your red blood cells. Infection with *Babesia* is called babesiosis. The parasitic infection is usually transmitted by a tick bite. Babesiosis often occurs at the same time as Lyme disease. The tick that carries the Lyme bacteria can also be infected with the *Babesia* parasite.

Bartonella — Several species of *Bartonella* bacteria cause disease in people. Infection with any one of these bacteria is referred to broadly as bartonellosis, although some forms of infection also have common names (for example, cat scratch disease). *Bartonella* bacteria are spread to humans by ticks, fleas, body lice, sand flies, mosquitoes, or contact with flea-infested animals. In the United States, the most common form of bartonellosis is caused by *Bartonella henselae*.

BCD — Buoyancy Control Device.

Biofilms — A biofilm comprises any syntrophic consortium of microorganisms in which cells stick to each other and often also to a surface.

CDC — Centers for Disease Control is the national public health agency of the United States. It is a United States federal agency under the Department of Health and Human Services.

COVID-19 — a contagious disease caused by a virus, the severe acute respiratory syndrome coronavirus 2 (SARS-CoV-2). The disease quickly spread worldwide, resulting in the COVID-19 pandemic

Dapsone Protocol — Dapsone is a drug that has been used since the 1940s to treat leprosy and a few other conditions. Dapsone combination therapy (DDS CT) is a novel drug regimen for the treatment of chronic Lyme disease. In a preliminary clinical trial of 100 patients, Dr. Horowitz gave Dapsone in combination with assorted other antibiotics and supplements. He found that patients reported significant improvement of ALL symptoms, except for headache.

Dive Master — A divemaster (DM) is a role that includes organizing and leading recreational dives, particularly in a professional capacity, and is a qualification used in many parts of the world in recreational scuba diving for a diver who has supervisory responsibility for a group of divers and as a dive guide.

Dyslexia — a learning disorder that involves difficulty reading due to problems identifying speech sounds and learning how they relate to letters and words (decoding). Also called a reading disability, dyslexia is a result of individual differences in areas of the brain that process language.

EKG — Electrocardiography is the process of producing an electrocardiogram (ECG or EKG), a recording of the heart's electrical activity through repeated cardiac cycles.

Endoscopies — An endoscopy is a procedure used to visually examine your upper digestive system. This is done with the help of a tiny camera on the end of a long, flexible tube.

GED — The General Educational Development (GED) tests are a group of four subject tests. It is an alternative to the US high school diploma,

HHS's "The Opportunity Project" — Olivia is the youngest inventor to participate in the U.S. Department of Health and Human Services, "The Opportunity Project" (TOP), a 14-week tech sprint with her app. TickTracker was selected by the U.S. Department of Health and Human Services as the "top tech tool" that is solving global health problems. Olivia presented her app at the White House and at the U.S. Census Bureau in 2019.

HHS — The United States Department of Health and Human Services (HHS) is a cabinet-level executive branch department of the U.S. federal government created to protect the health of the American people and provide essential human services.

Hypochondriac — A condition in which a person is excessively and unduly worried about having a serious illness. Hypochondriacs become unduly alarmed about any physical or psychological symptoms they detect, no matter how minor the symptom may be, and are convinced that they have, or are about to be diagnosed with, a serious illness.

IVs — An intravenous line (IV) is a soft, flexible tube placed inside a vein, usually in the hand or arm. Healthcare providers use IV lines to give a person medicine or fluids.

Judah and the Lion — Judah & the Lion are an American Alternative rock and folk band from Nashville, Tennessee, formed in 2011.

June Bug — The name "June bug" refers to any of the 100 species of beetles that are related to the scarabs familiar from ancient Egyptian iconography. Other common names for the June bug include "June beetle" and "May beetle." The common June bug is one-half to five-eighths inches long and reddish-brown in color. Being beetles, they also sport shiny wing covers, called elytra.

Kay Hagan Tick Act — is a bipartisan bill to provide assistance to combat the escalating burden of Lyme disease and other tick and vector-borne diseases and disorders. It was signed into law on December 20th, 2019. Named after the late

Senator Kay Hagan of North Carolina who died from the Powassan Virus that she contracted from a tick bite.

LivLyme Foundation — is a 501(c)(3) non-profit that was founded by Olivia when she was 12 years old. The LivLyme Foundation provides financial assistance to children and their families struggling with Lyme and other tick-borne diseases, while also supporting the work of researchers and scientists who are dedicated to finding effective treatments and cures for all tick-borne diseases and delivering tick education and awareness around the globe.

LonghaulTracker App — Invented by Olivia in 2022, LonghaulTracker is the first long haul-focused app that makes symptom tracking easy for any disease. This app provides a patient/user-driven data platform to assist patients and caregivers with not only tracking, but more importantly accurately communicating their symptoms in real-time.

Lyme Disease — Lyme disease is the most common vector-borne disease in the United States. Lyme disease is caused by the bacterium *Borrelia burgdorferi* and rarely, *Borrelia mayonii*. It is transmitted to humans through the bite of infected blacklegged ticks. The ticks that transmit Lyme disease can transmit other tick-borne diseases as well. Typical symptoms include fever, headache, fatigue, and a characteristic skin rash called *erythema migrans*. If left untreated, the infection can spread to joints, the heart, the nervous system, and other parts of the body, and can lead to chronic Lyme disease.

Lyme Disease Awareness Month — May is National Lyme Disease Awareness Month, a chance for Lyme patients, activists, and educators to spread information on how to prevent Lyme and tick-borne diseases.

Lyme Disease Challenge — The purpose of the Lyme Disease Challenge is to raise awareness and funding for improved Lyme disease diagnosis and treatment. The "Take a Bite Out of Lyme Disease" Challenge kicks off each May for Lyme Disease Awareness Month. You take a bite out of a lime and take a photo or video of your "sour face" then share a fact about Lyme disease and pass it on to three other people to take the challenge. Learn more at www.lymediseasechallenge.org.

Lyme Literate Medical Doctors (LLMD) — LLMD is a Lyme Literate Medical Doctor, a doctor trained in the diagnosis and treatment of Lyme and other tick-borne infections.

Lyme Spirochetes — Lyme disease is caused by a spirochete — a corkscrew-shaped bacterium called *Borrelia* that can bore deep into tissue, hide, and colonize. The Lyme spirochete is a uniquely opportunistic bacterium with an unusual ability to self-preserve. It can penetrate blood vessels and use the bloodstream to find tissues such as the brain, central nervous system, joints, organ, etc., to hide from immune responses and colonize in the host body.

MRI — A procedure that uses radio waves, a powerful magnet, and a computer to make a series of detailed pictures of areas inside the body.

National Western Stock Show — is an annual livestock show and festival held every January in Denver, Colorado since 1906. The stock show offers rodeos, livestock competitions, mutton busting, art shows, horse shows, and much more.

Olivia Goodreau Day — Colorado Governor John Hickenlooper named April 8th, 2017 "Olivia Goodreau Day" for being "one of Colorado's youngest and most impactful philanthropists, showing bravery and leadership that far exceeds her years. Whereas through her efforts with the LivLyme Foundation, Olivia is committed to increasing awareness of Lyme disease and to supporting scientists, doctors, and researchers as they work to improve treatment and find a cure."

Poison Ivy — is a type of allergenic plant in the genus Toxicodendron native to Asia and North America. If you come in contact with the ivy it can cause an allergic reaction rash from the oily resin on the leaves, stem, and roots of the poison ivy.

POTS — Postural Orthostatic Tachycardia Syndrome (POTS) is dysfunction of the autonomic nervous system that involves abnormal symptoms in many parts of the body, including abnormal blood flow to the heart, lungs, and brain. It often involves problems with digestion, temperature regulation, and many other involuntary functions of the body. POTS is a blood circulation disorder characterized by a specific group of symptoms that occur when standing upright and a heart rate increase from laying to standing. Because the condition involves the autonomic nervous system, which regulates mostly internal functions, it is commonly known as an "invisible illness."

Powassan Virus — is a tick-borne flavivirus that is related to some mosquito-borne viruses such as West Nile virus. Powassan virus is spread to people by the bite of an infected tick.

SnapChat — Snapchat is a multimedia instant messaging app and service for a fast and fun way to share the moment with your friends and family.

TBDWG — The Tick-Borne Disease Working Group was established by Congress in 2016 as part of the 21st Century Cures Act to provide subject matter expertise and to review federal efforts related to all tick-borne diseases, to help ensure interagency coordination and minimize overlap, and to examine research priorities. The focus of this effort is the development of a report to the Secretary of Health and Human Services and Congress on the findings and any recommendations of the Working Group for the federal response to tick-borne disease prevention, treatment and research, as well as how to address gaps in these areas. The Working Group is required to submit a report every two years, starting in December 2018 to 2022. Three reports have been sent to Congress in 2018, 2020, and 2022. The Tick-Borne Disease Working Group ended in December of 2022.

TedxTalks — A TEDx Talk is a showcase for speakers presenting great, well-formed ideas in under 18 minutes.

Tick-Borne Illnesses — Tick-borne diseases, which afflict humans and other animals, are caused by infectious agents transmitted by tick bites. Ticks can be infected with bacteria, viruses, or parasites. Some of the most common tick-borne diseases in the United States include Lyme disease, babesiosis, ehrlichiosis, Rocky Mountain Spotted Fever, anaplasmosis, Southern Tick-Associated Rash Illness, Tick-Borne Relapsing Fever, and tularemia.

TickTracker — Olivia invented the TickTracker App in 2018. TickTracker is the first global app that helps users track and report ticks in real time using geolocation. TickTracker app helps educate in the battle against tick-borne illness by letting the user see what ticks are around them in real time.

United States Air Force Thunderbirds — The air demonstration squadron of the United States Air Force (USAF). The Thunderbirds are assigned to the 57th Wing and are based at Nellis Air Force Base, Nevada.

Wilson's Disease — Wilson's disease is a genetic disorder in which excess copper builds up in the body. Symptoms are typically related to the brain and liver.

X-Ray — A penetrating form of high-energy electromagnetic ray.

Glossary of Tick-Borne Diseases in the United States

Alpha-Gal — Alpha-gal syndrome (AGS) (also called alpha-gal allergy, red meat allergy, or tick bite meat allergy) is a serious, potentially life-threatening allergic reaction. AGS is not caused by an infection. AGS symptoms occur after people eat red meat or are exposed to other products containing alpha-gal.

Anaplasmosis — *Borrelia miyamotoi* is a type of spiral-shaped bacteria that is closely related to the bacteria that cause tick-borne relapsing fever (TBRF). It is more distantly related to the bacteria that cause Lyme disease.

Babesiosis — *Babesia microti* is transmitted by the bite of infected *Ixodes scapularis* ticks — typically, by the nymph stage of the tick, which is about the size of a poppy seed. *Babesia* is a tiny parasite that infects your red blood cells. The tick that carries the Lyme bacteria can also be infected with the *Babesia* parasite.

Bartonella — Several species of *Bartonella* bacteria cause disease in people. Infection with any one of these bacteria is referred to broadly as bartonellosis, although some forms of infection also have common names (for example, cat scratch disease). *Bartonella* bacteria are spread to humans by ticks, fleas, body lice, sand flies, mosquitoes, or contact with flea-infested animals. In the United States, the most common form of bartonellosis is caused by *Bartonella henselae*.

Borrelia Mayonii — *Borrelia mayonii* are a type of bacteria recently found in North America that can cause Lyme disease.

Borrelia Miyamotoi — *Borrelia miyamotoi* is a type of spiral-shaped bacteria that is closely related to the bacteria that cause tick-borne relapsing fever (TBRF). It is more distantly related to the bacteria that cause Lyme disease.

Bourbon Virus — As of 2017, a limited number of Bourbon virus disease cases have been identified in the Midwest and southern United States. Some people who have been infected later died. Scientists continue to investigate possible symptoms caused by this new virus. Symptoms of people diagnosed with Bourbon virus disease included fever, tiredness, rash, headache, body aches, nausea, and vomiting. They also had low blood counts for cells that fight infection and help prevent bleeding

Colorado Tick Fever — Colorado Tick Fever (CTF) is a rare viral disease spread by the bite of an infected Rocky Mountain wood tick found in the western United States and western Canada.

Ehrlichiosis — Ehrlichiosis is the general name used to describe diseases caused by the bacteria *Ehrlichia chaffeensis*, E.

ewingii, or *E. muris eauclairensis* in the United States. These bacteria are spread to people primarily through the bite of infected ticks including the lone star tick (*Amblyomma americanum*) and the blacklegged tick (*Ixodes scapularis*).

Heartland Virus — Heartland virus is spread to people by the bite of an infected tick. Most cases have been reported from states in the Midwestern and southern United States.

Lyme Disease — Lyme disease is the most common vector-borne disease in the United States. Lyme disease is caused by the bacterium *Borrelia burgdorferi* and, rarely, *Borrelia mayonii*. It is transmitted to humans through the bite of infected ticks.

Powassan Virus Disease — Powassan virus disease is spread to people by the bite of an infected tick. Although still rare, the number of reported cases of people sick from Powassan virus has increased in recent years. Most cases in the United States occur in the northeast and Great Lakes regions from late spring through mid-fall when ticks are most active.

Rickettsiosis — Spotted fever group rickettsioses (spotted fevers) are a group of diseases caused by closely related bacteria. These bacteria are spread to people through the bite of infected mites and ticks. The most serious and commonly reported spotted fever group rickettsiosis in the United States is Rocky Mountain spotted fever (RMSF).

Rocky Mountain Spotted Fever (RMSF) — Rocky Mountain spotted fever (RMSF) is a bacterial disease spread through the bite of an infected tick. Most people who get sick with RMSF will have a fever, headache, and rash. RMSF can be deadly if not treated early with the right antibiotic.

STARI (Southern Tick-Associated Rash Illness) — A rash similar to the rash of Lyme disease has been described in humans following bites of the lone star tick, *Amblyomma americanum*. The rash may be accompanied by fatigue, fever, headache, muscle and joint pains. This condition has been named southern tick-associated rash illness (STARI). The cause of STARI is not known.

Tickborne Relapsing Fever (TBRF) — *Borrelia* bacteria that cause TBRF are transmitted to humans through the bite of infected "soft ticks" of the genus *Ornithodoros*. Soft ticks differ in two important ways from the more familiar "hard ticks" (e.g., the dog tick and the deer tick). First, the bite of soft ticks is brief, usually lasting less than half an hour. Second, soft ticks do not search for prey in tall grass or brush. Instead, they live within rodent burrows, feeding as needed on the rodent as it sleeps.

Tularemia — is a disease that can infect animals and people. Rabbits, hares, and rodents are especially susceptible and often die in large numbers during outbreaks. People can become infected in several ways, including tick and deer fly bites, skin contact with infected animals, drinking contaminated water, inhaling contaminated aerosols or agricultural and landscaping dust, and laboratory exposure.

In addition, people could be exposed as a result of bioterrorism. Symptoms vary depending how the person was

infected. Tularemia can be life-threatening, but most infections can be treated successfully with antibiotics.

Strains/variations of Lyme Disease —

Lyme - *Borrelia burgdorferi*

Lyme - *Borrelia afzelii*

Lyme - *Borrelia garinii*

Lyme - *Borrelia hermsii*

Lyme - *Borrelia lonestari*

Lyme - *Borrelia mayonii*

Lyme - *Borrelia miyamotoi*

Lyme - *Borrelia parkeri*

Lyme - *Borrelia recurrentis*

Tick-Borne Diseases Abroad —

African Tick Bite Fever

Boutonneuse Fever

Crimean-Congo Hemorrhagic Fever

Kyasanur Forest Disease

Lyme Disease

Mediterranean Spotted Fever

OMSK Hemorrhagic Fever

Tick-borne Encephalitis

References

Center for Disease Control and Prevention
www.cdc.gov

U.S Department of Health and Human Services
www.hhs.gov

Lymedisease.org
www.lymedisease.org

Lyme Disease Challenge
www.lymediseasechallenge.org

Mayo Clinic
www.mayoclinic.org

Hudson Valley Healing Arts Center
www.cangetbetter.com

Tick-Borne Disease Working Group
www.hhs.gov

Kay Hagan Tick Act
www.congress.gov

Healthline
www.healthline.com

John's Hopkins Medicine
   www.hopkinsmedicine.org

LivLyme Foundation
   www.livlymefoundation.org

TickTrackerApp
   www.ticktracker.com

The Opportunity Project
   www.opportunity.census.gov

Resources

To learn about the LivLyme Foundation, tick-borne diseases, find a Lyme Literate Medical Doctor, scientific Summits, LonghaulTracker App, Tickmojis, apply for a grant, news, and much more, visit www.livlymefoundation.org.

To learn more about Olivia's free Global App TickTracker, visit www.ticktracker.com.

To learn more about Olivia's latest app, the LonghaulTracker, which is a symptom tracking app to allow anyone suffering from any disease track and report their symptoms, visit www.longhaultracker.com.

Visit www.butshelooksfinebook.com to learn about the author Olivia Goodreau, book tour dates, events, and more.